YOU SAID IT,

PAUL HARVEY

YOU SAID IT,

PAUL HARVEY

Compiled by
LYNNE HARVEY

☆

Paulynne, Inc.

From the Television Series PAUL HARVEY COMMENTS
distributed by BING CROSBY PRODUCTIONS, INC. for
PAULYNNE PRODUCTIONS

Paulynne, Inc.

MEMO

To Paul Harvey

Darling:

What can we do about all those requests from listeners who want to read what you said on television?

The only thing I could think of was to put your COMMENTS together in a book.

Hope you approve.

Love,
Angel

TABLE OF COMMENTS

THE DISORDERLY PLANET

We don't expect the house to stay clean yet we expect the planet to stay tidy.

We recognize the necessity for unending dusting and periodic scrubbing and frequent repairing to keep the homestead presentable. Somehow we imagine that all the unkempt corners of the earth can be mopped up once and for all.

Any housewife knows she has but to put aside the broom and the place gets dirty again.

Any gardener knows he has but to put aside the hoe and the weeds take over.

Yet impatient Americans are inclined to expect prompt, total and final extermination of the world's malcontents.

Within any family there is intermittent ferment, friction, disagreement, dispute, discord. Include in-laws and there is sometimes bitterness.

Yet we are inclined to despair if the entire human family does not coexist in complete tranquillity.

This is what Lyndon Johnson was trying to say when he said, "This will be a disorderly planet for a long time."

He said, "We must deal with the world as it is, if it is ever to be as we wish."

Thus compared, good housekeeping with national policy, perhaps we may find our tedious chores in Korea and Vietnam and elsewhere less exasperating.

1

There is, however, a limit beyond which the most capable and healthy housewife may collapse.

Nor has Uncle Sam the energy or the resources to serve as custodian for the world.

Every empire which thus overextended itself, trying to put out all the fires and mop up all the mess, collapsed.

Therefore, if we can neither wet-nurse the whole world nor abandon all responsibility, we must learn to recognize our own limitations.

Infectious dirt on the doorstep—the Dominican Republic—must be cleaned up immediately and thoroughly.

Communist contamination of Cambodia, Indonesia, Pakistan: I don't think there is anything we could or should do about it.

Close to home again—Bolivia and Colombia? We must permit no more Cubas in this hemisphere.

If it sounds inconsistent to oppose communism in one hemisphere and not in another, then let's return to the parallel of the meticulous housewife. She opposes dirt, infection, contamination wherever it exists. She cannot eradicate dirt from the world; she can only fight it back from her own threshold.

What we must not forget is that the communists have a similar problem. Overextension is costly and debilitating for them, too.

The disquieting fact is that we have no choice but to keep on dusting and sweeping and mopping.

The harshness of the immediate picture is mitigated somewhat if we recognize that it was ever thus. Not in this world—if we truly deserve a better one—will we ever put aside the mop and the broom and the hoe.

WE ALL FEEL LIKE
REBELLING SOMETIMES

Experts in 1968 were assigned by the White House to interpret and explain the Los Angeles riots.

Experts named to committees and commissions in a dozen cities tried to answer, "Why?"

Experts from among social scientists, psychologists, criminologists, psychiatrists and politicians pretend to know the cause and some presume to prescribe a cure.

New York psychiatrist, Dr. Hector Ritey, blames "sex." He says, "In every country where whites and Negroes co-exist, the sexual issue is the underlying obsession."

Former Supreme Court Justice Charles Whittaker said we are "tolerating lawlessness when it is carried on under the name of civil rights." He urged stricter law enforcement.

Two University of Wisconsin sociologists contended that too strict law enforcement is what's causing the trouble. Doctors Arnold Silverman and Stanley Lieberson said, "Physical mistreatment, including police abuse, of Negroes, causes most race riots."

But since all the experts can't agree on the "why," let an amateur try. Me.

We all feel like rioting sometimes.

This, it seems to me, is the elementary fact which is overlooked by the theorists.

Hardly a day goes by but that each of us becomes exasperated, to some degree, by the slings and arrows of outrageous fortune.

Some real or imagined affront mobilizes our emotions.

A schoolteacher is "unfair" . . .

A colleague is "unkind" . . .

The employee is irked by some arbitrary management decision and management is antagonized by bureaucrats.

A thousand times, reading the biographies of those whom the world calls successful, I have been reminded that success is determined by how much you can dish out and more by how much you can take, how much crow you can eat, how often you can turn the other cheek—and somehow keep on keeping on.

Indeed, I suspect there are days when the President of the United States might feel like picketing the Senator from Oregon.

Sometimes futility, oft-times frustration, bedevils us all.

That which distinguishes you who "take it" and those who lash out at constituted authority is nothing more nor less than self-discipline.

"Rights" demonstrators recently have been marching in all directions: against school superintendents and in favor of pornography, against Vietnam and for home-rule in the District of Columbia. As fast as Congress insured one "right," new demonstrators erupted in the name of others.

So before we imagine that all the restlessness which flesh is heir to can be cured by race mixing or more laws or softer police or more money, let's remember there has always been fussing within the human family.

Among its children, fighting.

THE OLD COUNTRY

Youngster, let me tell you what it was like in the Old Country.

Once, milking an old cow in the back barn lot, I got tired of her swatting me in the face with a tail full of cockleburs.

So, with a piece of binder twine, I tied her tail to my leg.

I hadn't gone around the barn but about four times before I realized my mistake.

We had fun in the Old Country, though.

We played darts with a corncob. It had three chicken feathers in one end and a nail in the other. But if I picked the wrong target, like the sugar sack draining cottage cheese on the clothes line, Mom would likely thump me on the head with her thimble finger.

So we didn't have much of what you'd call juvenile crime in the Old Country.

Oh, every farm boy had to try smoking corn silk or grapevine once—until he got a mouthful of toasted ants—or until he got caught and got stropped.

And the grocer might fill the apple basket with the best ones on top.

But we didn't concentrate on learning the tricks of a trade; we learned the trade.

And stealing things or hurting people was almost unheard of in the Old Country.

My dad used to lend and to borrow money without security

or signature. Money changed hands, but it didn't change people.

Religion and education were all so mixed up together when I was a boy you couldn't tell where one left off and the other began. Patriotism was taught in every school class every day. Our national heroes were honored, almost revered.

Political speeches and religious sermons and civic celebrations always rang with patriotic fervor.

Soldiers were somebody.

Civil servants were servants, not masters.

Freeloading was a disgrace.

Ice cream was home made.

And marriage was forever . . .

In the Old Country.

A boy or girl could play alone in a public park on a summer night and nobody worried. Or they could play together and nobody whispered.

A farmer could plant anything he liked anyplace he wanted on his own land. Folks who worked harder were rewarded for it, so everybody worked harder.

Almost everybody had one idea about life: to leave the woodpile a little higher than he found it. Almost everybody did.

We had no card-carrying communists; we had Cross-carrying Christians . . . in the Old Country.

We told dialect jokes and everybody laughed, because all of us were "mostly something else," in the Old Country.

You asked me why I don't go back. Since I liked it so much, why don't I go back to the Old Country? I can't.

It isn't there anymore.

I am a displaced person, though I never left my homeland.

I am a native born American. I never left my country. It left me.

THE AMERICAN REVOLUTION AND

THE UN-AMERICAN REVOLUTION

"What's the difference," college-age audiences persist in asking me, "between yesteryear's dissenters and today's?"

The questioner goes on to recite how Patrick Henry and Nathan Hale and Tom Paine and their contemporaries were, in fact, revolutionaries. They opposed the establishment. They spoke out against it. They demonstrated against it. Eventually they opposed it with violence.

Yet we call them patriots while we call today's dissenters troublemakers.

"How come?" our young citizens want to know.

First, let's be sure to separate today's violent demonstrators from the non-violent protestors.

In a Constitutional Republic, we do not have to resort to violence to overthrow the establishment. We can overthrow it every election day.

So there is no justification whatever for today's agitators burning and looting their neighbors and openly advocating revolution, civil war.

Let us be careful, however, to consider separately those persons who oppose our Vietnam policy with proper petition and orderly demonstration. Those are entirely within their rights.

Many of today's young Americans feel sentenced to travel six thousand miles from home to "stop the advance of communism," yet if they dare try to stop it ninety miles from Florida they will be thrown in jail. Many consider this to be hypocrisy.

Further, the Neuremberg Trials of Nazi war criminals are predicated on the presumption that men should not contradict their principles—*even when ordered to do so.*

We have been executing and imprisoning assorted Nazis who insisted they were merely "following orders." But it was the judgment of humanity that they, ordered to massacre civilians, should not have followed orders.

Today many young Americans sincerely consider the Vietnam war to be a wanton massacre of innocent people, yet they are told they *must follow orders*—they must participate in the "massacre."

Because you and I understand each other, we can dare to discuss these apparent contradictions without being misunderstood.

Audiences of college-agers want straight answers.

We're asking them to die for their country; they want to know if it's worth it.

If they ask about the ruthless, violent, lawless demonstrations which profane our flag and destroy private or public property in the name of "rights," the answer is easy. Loyal Americans should stand together unalterably opposed to piracy.

But the morality of our official position in Vietnam is debatable, yet neither of the main line political parties offers an alternative.

Being old enough to fight and not old enough to vote is frustrating, anyway. When the most pertinent issue is not even on the ballot, what's left but desperation demonstrations?

I don't know the answer to that question, but I'll tell you this: Today's politicians better come up with the answers because tomorrow's voters are going to demand them!

8

ACCENT ON YOUTH

Less than a hundred years ago life expectancy in the United States was 38. A man was old at 35.

The American that age had raised a family and buried a wife. He rode a horse, same model every year.

On the range he bedded down between a cow and a campfire; on the farm he got up at four to haul water and fire-wood and tilled his field with a single-row plow.

But it was the women who had it hard. They not only had to put up with the pioneering, they had to put up with the pioneers.

They made their own soap, bread, clothes, did the washing, canning, helped in the fields, cooked for hired hands, bore more children than now and without anesthetic.

When a man's wife got sick, he didn't get on the telephone; he got on his knees.

They had no fancy names for sickness in the mountain, bush or brush country. You died of "fever" or you died of "colic" and you generally died young.

In the 1860's a man who craved education had to get it by firelight or by going to school after the youngsters were grown.

John Ben Sheppard of Texas retraced this history lesson with me and we reached the same conclusion: When our country was young, only the old were educated.

There was a saying in those days, "young men for war; old men for counsel."

That proverb hung on even after the reasons for it were gone.

Young men were pushed into the background; they were left out of professional and civic and governmental affairs until they were middle-aged.

They were not accepted at the conference table until they could sit two feet from it and still touch it with their belt buckles.

Today a man at 35 is young. Today life begins at forty, where it used to end.

Today's young man, in his Junior Chamber of Commerce, lives and works by idealistic principles deep-rooted in the American ism. His Creed speaks out for God, the brotherhood of men, economic justice and law and order and free enterprise and for service to humanity.

Today the young man does not wait for a still, small voice to challenge our conscience. He does it with a loudspeaker mounted on a truck.

Today's young man is not made for war, but for counsel.

I've seen them strengthen the backbone of a community which is falling apart from apathy and indifference.

I've seen local governments which would have been like wolves, except a few young men refused to be sheep.

Enterprises of great bulk and importance have been snatched from the brink of failure by a young hand which had never learned the gesture of defeat.

May God direct the energies of our uncommon, uncynical young men—leading them to whatever heights He will.

Yesterday's brave, brash young warriors might even be tomorrow's peacemakers . . .

If only because they don't know any better than to try.

10

BREAKING THE BRAIN BARRIER

It's not enough to point the way. Somebody has to *show* the way.

Since the Olympics of pre-history, the strongest, the bravest and the most fleet of foot hurled themselves against the objective of a four-minute mile.

Roger Bannister finally cracked that psychological barrier in June, 1954. Within two months John Landy did. Within ten years a dozen others.

My parents' generation believed man could never travel faster than sixty miles an hour or the wind would suck his breath away.

Barney Oldfield drove seventy. Now everybody does.

We waited through three and a half thousand years of recorded history to hurl anything into orbit about the earth. The Russians showed it could be done October 4, 1957. Within three months the United States duplicated their feat.

In 1967, for the first time, a doctor in South Africa transplanted a human heart. Within thirteen days, five hearts were transplanted.

For centuries men had predicted that it could and would be done but some one uncommon man had to run on ahead, reach out, bring the goal within the reach of the rest of us.

The Old Testament sought to point the way to heaven.

That was not enough. Christ had to show the way. "Follow me," He said.

Individuals move mountains in many ways, for better or worse.

One tenacious, persevering woman got prayers removed from all our public schools.

One determined, dedicated man forced the world's great car makers to make major modifications.

Five British girl typists, dedicated to the proposition that people should now help the country which has bankrupt itself helping them, offered recently to work an extra thirty minutes a day without pay. Five stenographers thus started a campaign which swept that nation and spread to Europe.

The most effective evangelist is the one who practices what he preaches.

The most successful business administrators are themselves on the job early.

The leader always has to be out front.

Further, to be examples worth following, you—your marriage—your business—demand tireless fence-mending and ceaseless improvement.

And your country.

Two-hundred years ago we Americans created a representative government so effective, so efficient that our American ism became the envy of the world.

Watching us, the entire enlightened world sought to imitate us.

It was after we became confused that they did.

The Republic, born in Philadelphia, needs to be born again.

Our American ism, revitalized, can again inspire the emulation of others. There is no easier way. We can't bribe them, force them, scare them. We have to show them.

We can lead only by example.

AMERICANS BAR WINDOWS

To armor plate your house as an answer to increasing crime is much like wearing rubber gloves as a remedy for a leaky fountain pen. Yet, while our High Court remains preoccupied with protecting the rights of the criminal at the expense of society, Americans have no choice but to surrender or to fight.

Many have elected to surrender. Many Americans who possess art treasures, coin or stamp collections, heirloom jewels —have buried them in bank vaults.

Others are electing to fight back against the rising tide of vandalism by fortifying their "new frontier" homes as Americans historically fortified their homes on the "old frontier."

Fortunately, as the criminals' weapons and tools have become more sophisticated, security devices have similarly improved.

Historically in our "wild west" natives constructed cliff-dwellings to protect their families and possessions from Navajo and Apache raiders.

Hopis farmed flatlands miles away from their mesa homes, for security.

The Spanish settlers built a defensive wall around what is now the city of Tucson. In the west of a hundred years ago, the army huddled inside stockades. Homes were constructed with small windows, a loft inside to hide livestock, a walled perimeter secured the house and its interior patio or courtyard.

When the Indian menace subsided, western Americans eagerly moved out into the open. For generations thereafter locks on doors were mostly ornamental and rarely felt a key.

It is this present generation which must accommodate a backward thrust of civilization.

In New York City, where half of our nation's drug addicts reside, most support their habit by stealing ten million dollars worth a day. There the masses huddle in apartments with electronically remote controlled entrances, automatically triggered recordings of barking dogs.

Phoenix, Arizona now has a major crime every 25 minutes. FBI figures show that Phoenix, with 26 burglaries a day, now leads the nation in that category of crime. Its Police Chief blames the fact that his force of lawmen is now spread too thin trying to police demonstrations of one sort or another.

While lawmen wrestle with the increasingly complex problems of waging brush fire warfare against the new breed of hit-and-run savages, we are witnessing a rebirth of an old-type architecture on the southwest horizon. Builders report increasing preference for smaller windows, "ornamental" iron grills, walled and guarded multiple-dwellings.

Some new homes are equipped with sliding steel panels buried in walls or roller-steel curtains concealed in attics. These steel shields may be drawn over windows and doors in the manner developed for protection of businesses in Europe, in North Africa and in our own riot-wracked cities.

Instinctively, many Americans react with repugnance to the idea of law abiding people retreating behind bars, surrendering the outside world to the lawless. But until the wilderness is re-tamed, the alternative is worse.

14

THE GOOD NEIGHBOR POLICY

Think for a moment of the one of your neighbors you like best. He may live across the street or next door or elsewhere in the block.

But the one neighbor you find most agreeable, most compatible, is not necessarily the one who heads every fund-raising drive.

Be honest now.

The neighbor you like best is not the community eager-beaver. He participates in community affairs, but his first concern is his own house, his own family.

Let's study him a moment and see what really comprises a good neighbor.

He keeps his own grass cut and his own house painted and he keeps his dog out of your garden. He treats his own family with affection and respect and sees to it they eat and dress as well as he can afford.

And he will buy gifts for his own with what's left over.

If your house catches fire and you shout for help, you know he'll be first to come running with a bucket.

But he will not volunteer uninvited services.

He will not inject himself into your family squabbles, he will not try to tell you how to run your own affairs. And he will not force money on you or presents on your wife.

In other words, the first requirement of being a truly "good neighbor" is *minding your own business!*

15

Keeping the family happy and his home attractive the good neighbor is an example that ultimately elevates the level of living of the entire community in which he lives.

Though we can readily recognize this basic truth in our own home communities, we somehow miss the point completely in our dealings with neighbor nations.

Injecting ourselves into the internal affairs of the others, forcing money and gifts on them, invites suspicion and resentment as surely as such conduct would alienate your neighbor next door.

We announce ourselves in favor of freedom for everybody.

But when the Algerians are willing to fight for freedom they have to fight American guns and American funds which we have provided to French troops.

How can we continue to meddle in the Middle East and avoid alienating factions?

In the South American nations which the Nixons visited, at least two of those governments came to power while the United States was financing the "other side."

We thus furnish ammunition to help the rabble-rousers rouse.

We strengthen the Communist charges of Yankee imperialism.

Such is the price we pay for involvement in the affairs of others. It is true in any neighborhood. The individual who is always snoopervising, eavesdropping, injecting himself or herself into others' affairs is the most despised of persons.

I had hoped the vilification heaped upon us during the Nixon visit might cause a reevaluation of our misplaced foreign aid.

It didn't.

We'll continue to pose as a good neighbor and behave as a bad one.

MARRIAGE VOWS

A lot of brides and grooms answer "I do," when they haven't really heard the question.

Some young folks and some not so young recite the marriage vows without paying attention to what they're saying.

Take the words, "In sickness and in health . . ."

It would seem that for a person to promise to be always faithful when there's sickness would be enough. But maturity and experience teaches us that's easy. It is more difficult to remain loyal and devoted in health when other distractions and temptations are more likely to intervene.

Take the phrase, "For richer or poorer . . ."

It seems superfluous to require that a person promise to live up to the marriage partnership when everything is going well.

When things are rough, when we're poor, have hard times, yes . . . then a man or woman should be required to stick with his bargain.

But "riches" . . . of course, one might assume any marriage would be certain to succeed if, as the songwriter says, "I have plenty of money and you . . ."

Not necessarily.

Do you happen to know the source of the marriage vows? Few do. The present wording of that marriage contract is not prescribed by Holy Writ. You'll not find it in the Bible. The framework of the words dates back to a primitive Sarum, England rite of 1078.

That formula evolved out of centuries of trial and error. Its workability is based on the experience of many generations, on honesty as much as on morality. We have learned that this code of human conduct is best.

Where it says "for richer or poorer . . ." we have learned that either is a strain on the tie that binds.

Daily we are confronted with examples of marriages which can survive and thrive in poverty, yet flounder and fall apart in prosperity.

The sweepstakes winner can be a happy workaday fellow until riches wreck his life.

It is true it seems of men and of nations. The children of Israel took forty years of hunger and privation and hardship, but they couldn't take it easy. So in their Promised Land of lush fruit and fat cattle and prospering flocks of sheep and milk and honey, they turned to evil and were consumed by it.

You know what I'd like to hear the clergyman say: "Dearly beloved, I don't think you know what you're getting into. So I am going to tell you something before I ask for your solemn promise.

"When I say in sickness and in health, I mean what that says! You're stuck! That means when you are fifty and suddenly feel like a young colt—you don't jump the fence!

"And when I say for richer or poorer, don't you say you do unless you mean to continue to love, honor and cherish—even if you strike it rich!

"Now, if you're sure you know what the vows say, and you are prepared to resist when health or riches tend to lure you astray, let's get on with the ceremony."

18

ONE WORLD NOT ENFORCEABLE

Black Africans are discriminating against brown Asians—chasing them out of Kenya a thousand a week.

As surely as the whites could not colonize the world, the browns can't either.

And reds can't either.

By the end of 1971, the sun will set on the once worldwide British Empire. The United Kingdom is withdrawing all military forces east of Suez.

Britain got rich by exploiting the world and then went broke trying to police it.

Prime Minister Wilson announced with "profound regret" that Britain is forced to abandon her longtime peace-keeping function in such places as Bahrein, Singapore and Malaysia.

The Prime Minister of Malaysia said, "We must immediately prepare to guarantee the safety of our nation."

With the British crutch removed they will stand alone—unless somebody goes running over there with another crutch.

If we do, we are inexcusably stupid.

If we can read and re-read history and fail to learn anything from it, then perhaps we deserve to follow Rome and Spain and Greece and China—which capsized and went down when their reach extended their grasp.

It is entirely likely that those fiercely nationalistic nations do not want American intrusion any more than they want British or Soviet or Red Chinese intrusion. They may tolerate our presence as long as our money holds out but their allegiance is not for sale.

The snafu in Vietnam—where the United States emerges, however inadvertently, as the "overwhelmer"—intended to reassure Asians. It has, instead, worried them.

Enlightened selfishness dictates that we must profit from Britain's immediate example and avoid over-extension. Our commitment to a "little war" in Vietnam has gradually involved us in one of the biggest wars we have ever fought.

Further, we have military commitments with forty other nations almost identical to the one which involved us in this untenable situation in Vietnam.

Britain is admittedly withdrawing from a major world role because of a balance of payments deficit, inflation and her gigantic homefront welfare burden.

Already, similar symptoms of weakness are apparent in the United States: balance of payments deficit, inflation and a gigantic homefront welfare burden.

The United States, richer than Britain and more nearly self-sufficient, will survive the drain and the strain longer. Still for us now just to follow Britain's decline, without even trying to avoid it, amounts to willful self-destruction.

That historically each great nation state has died by suicide should not hypnotize us. It should motivate us to take counter measures *now*. Britain might have been spared much pain if she'd accepted today's remedies yesterday.

We can be spared unnecessary agony tomorrow by accepting them now: reduced spending at home and abroad.

Let's stop being our brother's keeper. Let's start really being his brother—*and let him keep himself!*

THREE BILLION PEOPLE
ARE COMING TO DINNER

We live now in a world of three billion people. Half of them are undernourished or starving.

And world population is increasing so fast that there will be an additional three billion hungry pounding on our doors by the end of this decade.

What a terrible prospect. What an exciting challenge!

We have a date with desperation just thirty years away. In that thirty years we will have to learn to produce more food per acre and somehow to make more arable acres available.

Presently only 3% of our globe is food-productive soil.

In the past 25 years we've managed to expand the world's farmlands by only 15%.

Our economists are acutely concerned about America's diminishing supply of gold. Few appear concerned about the equally imminent food famine.

It is difficult for Americans, now fat, to comprehend the magnitude of this problem. Presently, compassionately, we are giving food away for products in kind to a hundred other nations.

Thus many of the world's people who would be forced to create additional farm production for themselves are encouraged to procrastinate.

Philosophers of the stature of Toynbee, anticipating a return to cannibalism in our time, are largely ignored.

I have boundless faith in the ability of ingenious Americans to overcome adversity. Historically, we are at our best with our backs to the wall.

You and I have seen technology create exciting new industries where nothing was before.

We have watched the awesome power of the atom unleashed, then broken to harness. Today it creates electricity, digs harbors, moves mountains.

We have developed television and its limitless potential for usefulness.

Orbiting satellites now offer communications and weather observation services and promise many more.

Jet planes make it possible for the uncommonest men to extend the range of their usefulness.

Computers, applied, accomplish in seconds that which might otherwise require months.

And each of these has showered the world with a fantastic fallout of fringe benefits.

Why, if man never succeeds in making use of the Moon—though I am confident he will—but if man never does—already, as a result of that effort, we are benefiting from an estimated 40,000 new inventions per year!

That is why I am challenged by the food crisis but not terrified by it.

We shall increase the world's food productivity per acre with chemical fertilizers and improved tools. We shall increase the world's arable acreage by irrigating with de-salinated sea water.

Indeed, we may perfect another pill, a suitable substitute for food.

But there is not time to waste. It's late in the afternoon and three billion people are due for dinner.

WHAT ARE FATHERS MADE OF

A father is a thing that is forced to endure childbirth without an anesthetic.

A father is a thing that growls when it feels good . . . and always laughs very loud when it's scared half to death.

A father is sometimes accused of giving too much time to his business when the little ones are growing up.

That's partly fear, too.

Fathers are much more easily frightened than mothers.

A father never feels entirely worthy of the worship in a child's eyes.

He's never quite the hero his daughter thinks . . . never quite the man his son believes him to be. This worries him, sometimes.

So he works too hard to try and smooth the rough places in the road for those of his own who will follow him.

A father is a thing that gets very angry when the first school grades aren't as good as he thinks they should be.

He scolds his son . . . though he knows it's the teacher's fault.

A father is a thing that goes away to war, sometimes.

He learns to swear and shoot and spit through his teeth and would run the other way except that this war is part of his only important job in life . . . which is making the world better for his child than it has been for him.

Fathers grow old faster than people.

Because they, in other wars, have to stand at the train station and wave goodbye to the uniform that climbs aboard . . .

And while mothers can cry where it shows . . . fathers have to stand there and beam outside . . . and die inside.

Fathers have very stout hearts, so they have to be broken sometimes or no one would know what's inside.

Fathers are what give daughters away to other men who aren't nearly good enough . . . so they can have grandchildren that are smarter than anybody's.

Fathers fight dragons . . . almost daily.

They hurry away from the breakfast table . . . off to the arena which is sometimes called an office or a workshop. There, with calloused, practiced hands they tackle the dragon with three heads: Weariness, Work and Monotony.

And they never quite win the fight but they never give up.

Knights in shining armor . . . fathers in shiny trousers . . . there's little difference as they march away to each workday.

Fathers make bets with insurance companies about who'll live the longest. Though they know the odds they keep right on betting. Even as the odds get higher and higher . . . they keep right on betting . . . more and more.

One day they lose.

But fathers enjoy an earthly immortality . . . and the bet's paid off to the part of him he leaves behind.

I don't know . . . where fathers go . . . when they die.

But I've an idea that after a good rest . . . wherever it is . . . he won't be happy unless there's work to do.

He won't just sit on a cloud and wait for the girl he's loved and the children she bore. He'll be busy there, too . . . repairing the stairs . . . oiling the gates . . . improving the streets . . . smoothing the way.

24

THE MAN AND THE BIRDS

The Christmas Story . . . the God-born-in-a-manger and all that . . . escapes some moderns. Mostly, I think, because they seek complex answers to their questions, and this one is so utterly simple. For the cynics, the skeptics and the unconvinced I submit a modern parable.

This is about a modern man. One of us.

He was not a Scrooge. He was a kind, decent, mostly good man. Generous to his family, upright in his dealings with other men. But he did not believe in all that Incarnation stuff which the churches proclaim at Christmas time. It just didn't make sense and he was too honest to pretend otherwise.

He just could not swallow the Jesus story. About God coming to earth as man.

"I am truly sorry to distress you," he told his wife, "but I am not going with you to church this Christmas Eve." He said he'd feel like a hypocrite. That he would much rather stay home. But that he would wait up for them.

He stayed. They went.

Shortly after the family drove away in the car, snow began to fall.

He went to the window to watch the flurries getting heavier and heavier, then went back to his fireside chair and began to read his newspaper.

Minutes later he was startled by a thudding sound. Then another, then another.

At first he thought someone must be throwing snowballs against his living room window.

When he went to the front door to investigate, he found a flock of birds huddled miserably in the snow. They had been caught in the storm and in a desperate search for shelter had tried to fly through his large landscape window.

Well . . . he couldn't let the poor creatures lie there and freeze.

He remembered the barn where his children stabled their pony. That would provide a warm shelter if he could direct the birds to it.

He quickly put on coat, galoshes. Tramped through the deepening snow to the barn.

He opened the doors wide and turned on a light.

But the birds did not come in.

He figured food would entice them in and he hurried back to the house, fetched breadcrumbs, sprinkled them on the snow, making a trail to the yellow-lighted wide-open doorway of the stable.

But to his dismay the birds ignored the breadcrumbs and continued to flop around helplessly in the snow.

He tried catching them.

He tried shooing them into the barn by walking around them waving his arms. Instead they scattered in every direction—except into the warm, lighted barn.

Then he realized they were afraid of him. "To them," he reasoned, "I am a strange and terrifying creature. If only I could think of some way to let them know they can trust me, that I'm not trying to hurt them, but to help them."

How?

Any move he made tended to frighten them, confuse them.

They just would not follow . . . they would not be led or shooed because they feared him.

If only I could be a bird myself, he thought.

If only I could be a bird and mingle with them and speak their language and tell them not to be afraid and show them the way to the safe, warm barn.

But I'd have to be one of them . . . so they could see . . . and hear and understand . . .

At that moment, the church bells began to ring. The sound reached his ears above the sounds of the wind.

He stood there . . . listening to the bells . . . Adeste Fidelis . . . listening to the bells pealing the glad tidings of Christmas . . .

And he sank to his knees in the snow.

MOD MOTHER, COME HOME
TO US NOW

Mother, dear Mother, come home to us . . .

A generation ago it was Father with whom you pleaded. Now you are the absentee without leave.

If we, your men, did this to you—we are sorry.

We want to duck the blame but we can't.

We want to blame the Russians or the Administration or television . . . or something . . .

But it was we who loved you as you were who made you what you are. It was we, Mod Mother, who enticed you to emaciation in the name of emancipation.

You had come so far since Helen of Troy and the Bible's Ruth; now you've gone further than we had intended.

Now, cooking by direction, eating by inspiration, you clutter the bowling alleys with beers and derrieres.

You parcel off your child to a sitting agency while you disguise your soft eyes with crayons and glue, replace your hair with somebody else's, squirm into skin-tight trousers and thus imitate us. That is not at all what we had intended.

Yet it was we, your men, who bought you your first bowling shirt. We lit your first cigarette. We boasted of your drinking prowess. We told you the unbecoming jokes that taught you that raucous laugh.

We ogled the tart and you mistook our ogling for admiration.

So you shortened your skirts and rolled your hair in toilet paper and wedged your kid into a grimy grocery cart and shopped the aisles looking for your lost femininity.

And so, my once-Fair Lady, we were your undoing. We lifted you down from the pedestal and made you this woeful creature, seduced before the vows and abandoned so soon after.

As wife you are bartered about for a night's entertainment in the so-called "social set." Your Aphrodites are Elizabeth and Mia and Jackie, and you lap up their private lives in tabloid print.

The pill is your ticket to a ride. Marriage and divorce are gossip cesspools. Childbearing, love and religion just get in the way.

But we who knelt to ask your hand or tie your shoe no longer even open doors for you—and it's we who miss that most.

Who takes time anymore to sit down with one of your sex and just let you talk about anything . . . else.

Now everything about you is "too" and "very." It leaves a flour-paste taste in our eyes.

We smell your perfumed sameness . . . we touch your prescription girdled girth . . . we kiss stale tobacco.

And we sleep restively. For we did this to you, Galatea. We made the comfortless bed we lie on, our Pygmallic coup with a Phyrric victory.

Perhaps it all began when you stood outside the tavern's swinging doors crying.

When we didn't come out, you came in.

Mother, dear Mother, come home to us now.

29

WE CANNOT LEGISLATE LOVE

Several members of Congress are sufficiently incensed over recent incidents of flag-burning that they are considering making desecration of our flag a federal offense.

Never has our flag meant so little to so many.

Two factors contribute to this increasing disrespect. One contributory cause is the fact which we have discussed previously: The press throws gasoline on these flames.

By focusing public attention on instances of shocking misbehavior, every youth determined to "shock" is provided with a sure-fire attention-getter.

Millions of Americans daily stand to salute, proudly display or otherwise honor this symbol of "the Republic for which it stands." But these are not news.

The one unwashed beatnik who makes a torch of our flag gets his picture in a thousand papers.

There is another sickness of our citizenry of which this flagrant disrespect is a symptom. It has to do with the fact that the Republic, itself, is less "respectable" than it once was.

You and I grew up in an era when patriotism was a two-way street. We defended our country and our country protected us.

It is not easy for us to comprehend the contradictions which confound today's school agers.

Their flag does not always protect them in foreign countries.

Indeed, today's American youth has been drafted to fight winless wars under a mongrel flag; wars which we were afraid to win and ashamed to lose.

Further, our nation, "with liberty and justice for all," now penalizes the hard workers, subsidizes the lazy.

Our nation orders our sons to travel six thousand miles from home to prevent the advance of Communism . . . yet they are told to tolerate that same menace just ninety miles from Florida.

You and I have been around longer and we can rationalize that our Republic, for all its imperfections, is still the best there is. But our still idealistic sons and daughters see a lecherous fugitive from justice re-elected to the Congress and Old Glory hangs limp and soiled over our nation's Capitol.

I am not defending them. I am trying to help explain some of their disdain for the values you and I treasure.

A House Judiciary Subcommittee considered an assortment of new laws against misuse of our flag. Some would prescribe penalties of ten thousand dollars and five years in prison.

Resentment in Congress is being called a "patriots' back-lash."

"We'll teach those young hooligans they'd better respect our flag or else!"

There should, indeed, be a penalty for flagrant expressions of disrespect. Yet we should have learned by now that love cannot be legislated.

In Congress, before all this steam blows off in the whistle, perhaps our energies should be directed toward correcting the hypocrisies and inconsistencies which discredit our ism.

While we're singing "God Bless America," let's give youngsters some good reason why they should.

LBJ IS NOT THE USA

Young Americans are being told that being an American is worth dying for and, what is sometimes more difficult, worth working for. They're not sure it's worth it.

I'm on high school or college campuses somewhere every week. I hear many school-agers professing disenchantment with the American ism when actually they are merely in disagreement with the incumbent administration.

The American ism and the incumbent administration, whichever administration occupies the White House and controls the Congress, are two different things.

This important distinction must be made clear before angry young rebels further profane our flag when their grievance should instead be directed at temporarily elected politicians.

The American ism, if imperfect, is still the best available. Our Constitution, even carelessly patched and sometimes misinterpreted, is still the best blueprint for an orderly existence.

If it is by our "fruits" that we are to be judged, the American ism has borne such bountiful fruits that our six per cent of the earth's people produce more than all five of the other big six nations combined.

Despite the continuing internal friction resulting from ceaseless social adjustment, our individual standard of living is higher and wider than anywhere else on Planet Earth.

The problems which bedevil this generation of Americans

demand further adjustment of our relationships with one another and with the world, but there are provisions in our Constitution for the orderly accomplishment of that objective.

Some young Americans are searching for some other "ism" when they should be applying themselves to the perpetuation and refinement of our own.

Most frequently I hear them criticize:

1. A "government" which penalizes people who profit and prosper in order to subsidize laziness, indigence—even promiscuity.

2. A "government" which sends us off to fight foreign wars under a mongrel flag, with less than our best weapons, where the announced objective is a stalemate on the fifty yard line; wars which we appear ashamed to lose yet somehow afraid to win.

3. A "government" which tells us we might have to go six thousand miles from home, perhaps to die trying to stop the advance of communism—yet if we dare try to do anything about it ninety miles from Florida we'll be thrown into jail.

To keen, young intellects these inconsistencies amount to hypocrisy. They indict the "government," some renounce our country, burn our flag.

There is nothing in our Constitution nor in our Declaration of Independence nor in any of our several State Constitutions which can properly be blamed for these grievances. They derive from the administration of our affairs in the hands of present and past leaders.

Let us ventilate our righteous wrath, but let's not miss the target.

Our American ism has failed us in no way; too frequently we fail it.

UNCLE SAM AND HIS

SPOILED BRATS

Uncle Sam represents you and me—all of us—collectively.

Surely, as if he were a real "uncle," he wants only the best for us.

Surely, therefore, he must now be asking himself, "What did I do wrong?"

Kentucky tobacco growers pay $30 a day wages for unskilled tobacco cutters.

Every harvest morning growers' trucks drive up to the unemployment office in Lexington, Kentucky offering long lines of unemployed welfare recipients $30 for six hours work. Very few accept.

Most insist "that's not my line of work," and thus they legally perpetuate their parasitic existence.

How many such persons might—denied a handout—be motivated to become productive and eventually prosperous—there is no way to know.

But this we can measure: Welfare roles continue to increase twice as fast as our population is increasing.

In New York City, 14,000 additional welfare recipients are added to the roles each month.

Welfare recipients have organized themselves into pressure groups demanding increased handouts. There is in New York a Citywide Coordination Committee of Welfare Groups seeking "to coordinate efforts of all the groups."

Nationally, there is the "National Welfare Rights Organization," which is tantamount to a union through which welfare recipients can channel some of their welfare dollars to paid lobbyists in Washington where they can demand more of your money. This NWRO claims to represent 200 affiliated groups in 35 states. Members flood welfare offices with applications for more aid and stage rallies, picket lines and sit-ins when they don't get "what we are entitled to."

Uncle Sam's well-intentioned generosity has spawned a generation of spoiled brats and the longer a baby is on Pablum—the more he cries at the weaning.

Any parent who remembers sweating for what he wanted is instinctively inclined to want things to be easier for his children—but history says of men and nations that ease most often breeds restiveness.

The fathers of our Republic knew better than to promise to provide happiness. They guaranteed your right "to pursue happiness"; there's an important difference.

That is your right: To "pursue" it, not to "purloin" it.

Historically, the fact that others had more was an inspiration to Americans to work harder, loaf less, reach higher, improve themselves.

Is it possible . . . is it really possible that, despite all our enlightenment, politicians can still buy our votes . . .

. . . *with our money!*

WHAT IS A POLICEMAN?

Don't credit me with this mongrel prose. It has many parents, at least 420 thousand of them: policemen.

A policeman is a composite of what all men are, a mingling of saint and sinner, dust and deity.

Culled statistics wave the fan over stinkers, underscore instances of dishonesty and brutality because they are "news." What that really means is that they are exceptional, unusual, not commonplace.

Buried under the froth is the fact: Less than one-half of one per cent of policemen misfit that uniform.

That's better average than you'd find among clergymen.

What is a policeman? He, of all men, is at once the most needed and the most wanted.

He's a strangely nameless creature who is "Sir" to his face and "fuzz" behind his back.

He must be such a diplomat that he can settle differences between individuals so that each will think he won.

But . . .

If a policeman is neat, he's conceited; if he's careless, he's a bum.

If he's pleasant, he's a flirt; if he's not, he's a grouch.

He must make instant decisions which would require months for a lawyer.

But . . .

36

If he hurries, he's careless; if he's deliberate, he's lazy.

He must be first to an accident and infallible with a diagnosis.

He must be able to start breathing, stop bleeding, tie splints and, above all, be sure the victim goes home without a limp. Or expect to be sued.

The police officer must know every gun, draw on the run and hit where it doesn't hurt.

He must be able to whip two men twice his size and half his age without damaging his uniform and without being "brutal."

If you hit him, he's a coward; if he hits you, he's a bully.

A policeman must know everything—and not tell.

He must know where all the sin is—and not tell.

He must know where all the sin is—and not partake.

The policeman must, from a single human hair, be able to describe the crime, the weapon and the criminal—and tell you where the criminal is hiding.

But . . .

If he catches the criminal, he's lucky; if he doesn't, he's a dunce.

If he gets promoted, he has political pull. If he doesn't, he's a dullard.

The policeman must chase bum leads to a dead end, stakeout ten nights to tag one witness who saw it happen—but refuses to remember.

He runs files and writes reports until his eyes ache to build a case against some felon who'll get dealed-out by a shameless shamus or an "honorable" who isn't.

The policeman must be a minister, a social worker, a diplomat, a tough guy and a gentleman.

And of course he'll have to be a genius . . .

For he'll have to feed a family on a policeman's salary.

YOUR UNCLE SAM,
LAST OF THE BIG SPENDERS

Nikolai Lenin said it: "Germany will militarize herself out of existence, England will expand herself out of existence, America will spend herself out of existence."

Your Uncle Sam apparently intends to fulfill that 1917 prophesy.

Conscientious money managers in Congress have been pleading with the White House: "Please cut spending!"

The administration's reply was: "Raise taxes; bring in more money!"

The White House implied that increased federal income would tend to balance our outgo, retard inflation. There is no evidence your increased taxes would be used for the purpose.

The likelihood, based on past and present performance, is that Sam would just continue and accelerate his spending spree.

Taxpayers have been more than generous. Over the past ten years your federal taxes increased 95%, which is faster than our total economy has grown.

During that same decade—while your taxes were increased 95%—federal government spending increased 112%.

In 1960 the federal government budget was $94 billion. Last year it was $172 billion. Last year the President asked $186 billion.

There has been a lot of talk about Administration economizing. Yet, while former President Johnson turned off some White House lights to save electricity, 112 new federal projects have been launched since 1960. Sixteen more new ones were requested in 1968.

Since 1960 only one federal program has been abolished, all others have been increased.

When American tourists were asked not to go abroad to keep our dollars at home, Hubert Humphrey promised Ivory Coast Africa another $36½ million.

The *Arizona Republic,* citing contradictions between what the White House says and what it does, recently noted that when Lady Bird spent millions of your dollars to beautify highways . . . at the same time another agency of government spent $5 million putting up roadside signs!

You were paying the salaries of 276,000 more federal employees in 1968 than in 1967.

Even ending the war will not end Sam's extravagant binge.

The war is blamed for increased federal spending when the fact is that non-military spending has almost doubled in the past eight years.

Income tax time is the time to be reminded that those are your dollars.

Any election year is the time to demand your Congressman recognize that fact, too. Congress holds the purse strings. Congress has the power to regulate extravagant Sam's allowance.

A courageous handful on Capitol Hill will demand that any federal tax hike must be predicated on reduced federal spending. Encourage them . . .

Or else, silent when you should protest, you acquiesce to Lenin's prophesy that "America will spend herself out of existence."

THE SUBSTITUTE RELIGIONS

Take one God away from a man and he'll create another.

Man, inescapably aware of his finite inadequacy, must worship something bigger than himself.

Robert Ruark wrote that the white man was responsible for African ferment, "because we took away the native's historic tribal rites and failed to replace those with something of value."

Similarly, recently our churches have so compromised themselves that many youngsters, disillusioned and confused, are grasping at spiritual straws.

A bearded guru from India made tremendous impact on America and England because he appeared to fill the void which was left when our churches began to "tolerate" everything.

Both membership and attendance in America's main-line churches are lagging behind our population increase.

Gallup Survey shows 92% of Americans believe "religion is important," but only 60% belong and only 30% attend!

They know what they need, but they aren't getting it in Church!

Meanwhile cults are flourishing.

One Indian philosopher advocates a system of "meditation" which leads to "blissful consciousness." His system, he says, "also will eliminate wars, famine and earthquakes."

When Mia Sinatra flew back to India with him, Maharishi Mehesh Yogi expressed confidence that she would make a "good disciple" and promised to guide her to "higher spiritual experience."

At the same time, Buddhism has twice as many disciples in the United States as it did just two years ago. No "regular church" can claim such a spectacular growth rate.

What's the matter? What happened to diminish its influence? Church attendance stagnates, while crime, licentiousness, promiscuity, divorce and social disease pyramid.

Clergymen, disillusioned with the ineffectiveness of the Church, rebel—openly or clandestinely.

Some of us who are convinced that God and the devil are at war in our world see Satan winning every battle!

Those who argue that this upheaval constitutes nothing more serious than an accelerated social evolution are refuted by the fact that their liberal ism is bearing much bitter fruits: crudeness, rudeness, violence, pornography, rebellion.

Our streets are unsafe even for policemen!

So the drift away from what we used to call "fundamental religion" has not been, in any way, beneficial.

We can continue on course and destroy the few remaining "absolutes" of our churches. We can disregard moral law and discredit civil law.

But when we have done our utmost to make sure "God is dead," He will rise again.

Men, left to their own devices, make such an unholy mess of society and such a despair and disease-wracked wreckage of themselves—that eventually, driven to their knees, they resume praying for the very spiritual guidance which they sought with such determination to dilute and destroy.

THE CANNIBAL SOCIETY

America has become a cannibal society, devouring its best.

The competents, numerically outnumbered by the incompetents, are being coralled, restrained, confined and milked like barnyard cattle.

The giants who created our skyscraper civilizations are now ordered to obey Lilliputian bureaucrats.

Common men—who owe their jobs to uncommon men who create jobs—gang together to shackle their providers.

Americans are becoming congenital dependents. Even as loafing relatives extort a livelihood by claiming they have a "right" to your money—so today eight million homegrown moochers, insist that *you are responsible for their welfare!*

Thus we subsidize promiscuous mothers and their illegitimate babies and lazy featherbedders and goldbricking government payrollers . . . while we penalize the strong, the purposeful, the productive with disproportionate burdens of taxes, pressures, red tape.

We praise ventures which are "non-profit" and grant them tax advantages and social acceptance, yet we damn the men who make the profits which make the "non-profit" ventures possible.

Americans want to keep the electric lights but destroy the generators.

What if the men of brains and initiative and industry should go on strike? It happened once. The Dark Ages were a period of stagnation when men of exceptional ability gave up, figured "what's the use," even went underground—for a thousand years.

Ayn Rand, author of "Atlas Shrugged," thinks it may have to happen that way again.

Dr. Charles Mayo says, "I know of no individual, no nation, that ever did anything worthwhile on a five-day week."

Already many American industrialists are turning the keys on their corporations and going to Florida—either part-time or full-time—to become non-productive beachcombers.

Curiously, Russia is beginning to reward the uncommon men. Soviet scholar, Vadim A. Trapeznikov—not without Kremlin sanction—is now referring to the Soviet system as "obsolete." He says Russia's economy must now rely on the "more productive profit motive."

We, on the other hand, continue to play the democratic con game which pretends that all men are equal and that anybody who demonstrates any inequality should be punished for it.

Any insolent beggar can wave his sores in your face and plead for help in the tone of a threat. You are expected to feel "guilty" for having more than he.

Any barefoot bum from the pestholes of Asia or Africa cries out, "How dare you be rich!" and we beg him to be patient and we promise to give it all away as fast as possible.

The economic creed of "enlightened selfishness" which made our nation the powerhouse of this planet has been so maligned that now it sounds like heresy when I say:

Any man who claims you owe him a living is a cannibal. Whether foreign or domestic, he is a cannibal.

If you choose to help him, that is one thing.

If he demands your "help" as his "right," he is a leech, a sycophant, a parasite. He is a cannibal seeking to survive by consuming you.

43

WHY DON'T THE PSYCHOLOGISTS

SPEAK UP?

We are being told that "colonialism" is another word for "paternalism" as if that were bad.

Workers are being told that their quarrel is with the bosses.

Minorities are struggling to wrest themselves free from "domination."

School-agers are resisting the authority of parents, police and school officials.

Churchmen rebel against their own heirarchy; some, indeed, deny God Himself.

In the midst of all this misplaced trendency toward anarchy, our psychologists are unexplainably silent. Students of human behavior are aware that we all need to submit to an authority that's bigger than ourselves; why don't they speak up and spare us this turbulence, frustration, and torment?

The jungle native, denied the paternalism of enlighted leaders, will adopt the witch doctor.

Communists, who reject the paternalism of God, substitute an earthly dictator, the State.

Every experiment with insignia-less uniforms in all military history has led us back to recognition of the fact that soldiers must have officers and the officers must be obeyed.

In business, whenever we've tried running the office or shop without a "boss," the result has been chaos.

44

Social clubs and fraternal organizations have no need other than a psychological need for a "commander," a "president" or "a grand exalted imperial potentate."

Children need and want parental authority to feel secure. Denied this authority, they will misbehave until the policeman serves that function.

Presently, many Americans and others are demanding to be free of paternalism without knowing what they are talking about.

Much resentment presently resulting in street rioting is not race based; it derives from failure of today's free wheeling, freedom seeking citizens to understand themselves.

Americans did not come to America in the first place to be "free."

They prayed, *"Thy will* be done on earth." They bound themselves to God's will—and prospered.

We, demanding to be "free," have become unguided missiles hellbent for nowhere.

Historically, if men have no God they will create one.

If men have no leader, they will select, elect or submit to one.

Why don't the psychologists speak up and end this futile quest for "equality" before we wreck this splendid social order in which all men are free to be unequal.

We don't really want all that our slogans demand.

On the first day of Kindergarten, a teacher asked each pupil what he wanted to be when he grew up.

One five-year-young lad was very definite. "When I grow up," he said importantly, "I'm going to be a lion tamer. I will have lots of fierce lions. I will walk into the cage and they will all roar . . ."

He stopped, hesitated, then added, "Of course, I'll have my mommy with me."

LOVE BY DEGREES

Love is a living thing. It grows or it dies.

In the beginning, romance. Boy and girl. Man and woman. The breathless ecstasy of infatuation. The honeymoon. The excitement of exploration and discovery.

Then, as with all growing things, one day the bloom is wilted. The seeds have fallen from the pod to propagate anew. And in the less than thrilling middle years, there is a time when married folks just sort of tolerate each other.

Finally, much later than most realize, love sets in.

Real, whole, complete love—in the third degree.

Unfortunately, in that sometimes uncomfortable in-between time, uncomfortable mostly because it is his own waning virility which a man despises—and for a woman, her wrinkles —some fly the coop, jump the fence, seek to re-cycle their lives and rediscover romance.

But in starting over they are delaying the ultimate fulfill-ment, for full-grown love requires many seasons.

Thus, in human relations, love evolves.

It is somewhat the same with the love of a man for his home.

To a boy, the home town is filled with excitement and discovery.

To the young man, far horizons beckon.

But the old man, if he is still seeking far horizons, is a

piteous person—uprooted, chasing every place, loving no place.

On the other hand, some of the happiest persons I have ever known either returned to their home towns or tolerated their home towns through the long, dull years when restlessness might have lured them elsewhere. Finally, they developed a fierce pride in their community, a determined, protective permanent love in the third degree.

Perhaps with nations, too, this evolution can neither be hurried nor denied.

The revolution's fever and fire once spent, the nation becomes complacent, then crotchety and self-critical.

In our United States, with the honeymoon behind us and love in the third degree yet unrealized, we are inclined to carp and criticize and condemn and blame the government and even flirt with other kinds.

I hope we don't jump the fence seeking greener pastures in our middle years. For this, with nations as with men, is merely to start over again.

A GIRL IN KANSAS CITY

Young years ago in the Pacific left me with an undulating appetite for Polynesian, Malayan and Oriental food. Stateside, Cantonese cooking is a reasonable facsimile. This is not about that.

But during a recent visit to Kansas City I learned that such cuisine was available just down the street and downstairs from the Muelbach; I went.

Early to bed means early to eat so I was alone in the simulated tropical setting or I might not have noticed the next four customers.

They were a man and wife, comfortable, respectable—a crew-cut son wearing horn-rimmed glasses—

—and the girl.

She, like the young man, was eighteenish, self-conscious. Her white and gray lace blouse becomed her, neat, pretty. The white bow in her hair belonged there. Her face glowed softly with round-eyed innocence. If that innocence were contrived, which I doubt, more the pity.

I am not usually a people-watcher, except with professional purpose. I am never an eavesdropper—except with professional purpose. But part of what ensued in words and gestures could not have escaped my notice.

"What shall we have to drink, dears?" the mother asked.

The large menu was decorated with three-color sketches of

such exotic rum-base cocktails as "Hula Punch," "Voo Doo," "Navy Grog," "Heavenly Flower" and "Secret Kiss—limit two!"

From my rattan table across the room the girl's hesitancy was apparent. Her wish to make a favorable impression on the more sophisticated prospective in-laws was also apparent.

Though few of the words reached my ears, the smiles of reassurance and the nods of acquiescence affirmed that, "These are very mild drinks, you know, hardly more than soda pop . . ."

And there was a skillful assist from the waitress; surely I only imagined her reluctance.

So each of the four was served something tall and frosty and colorful with a straw protruding through a cone of ice and a garnish of mint leaves and fruit peel and a bright red maraschino cherry.

Three drank. She sipped. I hurt.

The girl in Kansas City was really not my rightful concern. I'd never seen her before and I'll not likely see her again except in indelible recollection.

For in the unfolding of this significant little drama—midst phony palm fronds and simulated bamboo curtains and gaudy paper lanterns and pagan carvings and recorded music—another generation was being subtly seduced by the artfully camouflaged trouble which always starts out seeming fun.

Her soft, girlish laughter was louder as I left. She was eating. The glass of "Heavenly Flower," or whatever it was—its ice melted, its mint leaves wilted, its straw soggy, its cherry missing—was mostly still there. It was about one-third empty.

It would be easier next time.

MAKE SURE YOU'RE DEAD

Before they start to transplant parts of you into the body of somebody else, make sure you're dead.

There is presently no single accepted medical standard for determining when a dead person is dead, and with the increase in human transplants it is now imperative that we find one.

In June of 1964, a plane crash victim was brought into Cooley Dickinson Hospital in Northampton, Massachusetts with no pulse and no blood pressure. By some accepted clinical standards he was dead.

That man is now Senator Ted Kennedy.

Sometimes, right in the middle of life, along comes the smiling mortician.

In Auckland, New Zealand last April a year-old baby drowning victim was brought ashore by boat as a corpse—and is still alive.

Tavern owner James Keemer of Powellsville, North Carolina shot "to death" earlier this year—is back at work.

Mrs. Charlotte Mayer, Chicago mother found hanged in the boiler room of her apartment, had no breath, no pulse, was declared "dead" by the Fire Department ambulance crew—but was revived.

University of Missouri coed, Glanda Gampher, found in a city park, declared "dead" at the city morgue, was being prepared for autopsy when she "came back to life." That she did die three days later might be blamable on the delay in efforts to revive her.

All these incidents I recall from just the past year. I have a file full of documented cases dating back several years.

Battlefield doctors are similarly without any certain criteria for determining death. Specialist Jacky Bayne was pronounced "dead" at a field hospital in Vietnam a year ago. He was taken to a temporary morgue. Graves registration section was routinely advised. The embalming procedure had begun before an alert embalmer detected a feeble sign of life. Jacky Bayne is now back home, not fully recovered. Because medics were unnecessarily delayed in getting the blood pumping, his brain was damaged.

Lorene Hawks of Dallas, 51, has "died" 152 times. Each time with electric shock and heart massage she was revived.

Jockey Ralph Neves, once pronounced "dead" after a bad racing spill, recovered to ride many more winners.

In Glasgow, Scotland Mrs. Catherine Leask was sent from the Royal Infirmary to the morgue, certified "dead." As an ambulance man was leaving her on the slab he noticed a quiver in her neck. He applied oxygen from ambulance equipment; she is alive.

For every "dead" person who was subsequently revived, with or without brain damage due to delay, no one knows how many more were killed by the embalmer or buried alive.

Medically, there is no universally agreed upon standard for determining when life ends. With our increasing interest in transplanting beating hearts and other functioning organs, we'd best determine a standard before some grizzly scandal discourages further transplants and discredits medicine per se.

TO DREAM THE IMPOSSIBLE DREAM

Young people are trying to tell us something. Some, frustrated by our unwillingness to listen, to our inability to comprehend what they are trying to say, deduce that there can be no communication between the generations. Some react violently, some more patiently.

When the World Council of Churches met in Uppsala, Sweden a group of young Christians pleaded with their elders to break with the status quo and to help find nonviolent paths to social change.

Enlightened young, disillusioned by a generation of parents who too often talk one way and act another, demand re-examination of some of the tarnished old truths.

I am not sure how much of this new introspection is good; I am sure it is inevitable.

More than ever, young people are rushing on ahead where their elders fear to tread.

Granted, some of the young rebels are sick. Some are the soft, pithy, tasteless fruit which fell from an over-nourished family tree.

Others are responsible critics of contemporary mores and antiquated preconceptions.

They include young Columbuses determined to explore the unexplored, young Wright brothers, young Tom Edisons, young Tom Paynes, young Ben Franklins, young men and women always daring to dream the impossible dream.

And young Fidel Castros, too.

Some may rip to shreds much of the good fabric of our social order in their anxiety to prove or to disprove, each to his own satisfaction.

There is enough admitted hypocrisy, pomposity and imperfection among their parents to justify some of this unwillingness to go along with things as they are.

Our performance has not always matched our nobler protestations; perhaps theirs won't, but let's give the responsible restless young a respectful audience.

A schoolager named Jerry Anderson of Huntington, Tennessee recently wrote:

"Ha Ha!" they laughed, "he's at it again, the silly fool!
"Come see the show, come one and all,
Watch the village idiot racing toward a fall."

Out in the meadow the fool ran 'round,
Leaping and jumping and flapping his arms;
Trying to gain speed so's to get off the ground.

"Please don't laugh," said a little girl.
"He means no harm, he's trying to fly."
"He's insane!" came the haughty reply.

The villagers laughed 'til the sun was low,
They were still laughing when sunset came.
Tears filled their eyes, they'd been laughing so.

Then suddenly the laughter stopped.
Men gaped, women fainted, the little girl was crying . . .
For out there over the meadow the fool was no longer running;
He was flying!

HIGHER, HIGHER THE WALL!

The Berlin Wall, intended to keep communism's captive humans captive, hasn't.

In seven years 3,500 East Germans have escaped. They went over, under or around the wall.

At the same time 499 of the Wall's guards have left their posts and fled to freedom.

So the communist boss of Red East Germany, Walter Ulbricht, reinforced the wall. He planned row after row of obstacles—nine rows—each progressively more difficult.

In East Germany and wanting out, first you will have to surmount two fences, each five feet high and topped with barbed wire.

The second fence is electrically wired to set off alarms at the slightest touch. At the sound of the alarm guards are alerted, floodlights lighted.

If you should surmount the electric fence, you are in an open dog run where 247 trained-to-be-vicious dogs prowl constantly. The night time escapee may trip over hidden wires which are rigged to trigger flares.

By now the fugitive is under glaring searchlights and Russian made machine guns. Ulbricht designated 15,000 border guards, each ordered to shoot to kill.

A few steps farther is an asphalt pavement patrolled by armored vehicles. They race up and down the border so precisely timed that every open area is always in view to at least two—one approaching from each direction.

In the very unlikely event that the escapee gets past this point, he enters an area of plowed earth. Beyond that a steep-sided ditch will trap any who might seek to escape in a military tank.

And this is not all!

If a fugitive gets past the three fences and the electric wires and the trip-wires and the dogs and the machine guns and the patrol vehicles and the armed guards and the ditch—his final dash must be made across an open one-hundred feet covered with cinders where powerful mercury vapor lamps make even the most fleeting figures an easy target for tower guards.

And the open area is studded with six-inch steel spikes.

If we can imagine that some would-be escapee could surmount all these obstacles and get this far—

Then he has reached the wall!

But he will discover that the Berlin Wall has been made higher. Now there is a large pipe along the top, fifteen inches in diameter, making any hand-hold impossible.

Ulbricht has his new "modernized border," as he calls it, one-third completed. He expects to have the entire 99 mile wall thus reinforced and ringing West Berlin by 1970.

The United States of America, for all its imperfections, is still the only nation in the world where people are standing in line waiting to get in . . . instead of crawling through barbed wire and over stone fences or braving stormy seas in small boats—dying—trying to get out.

The defense rests.

RE-VITALIZE VETERANS'
ORGANIZATIONS

Recall to arms! Men of the Argonne, Chateau Thierry, Belleau Wood—this is a call for volunteers.

The goof-offs among a younger generation, trying to hide wet ears with long hair, desperately need guidance. Not somebody to "point" the way—somebody to "show" the way.

You're it!

Men of the Belgian Bulge and Guadacanal . . .

Men of Normandy, Metz and Porkchop Ridge . . .

You who thought you'd won your time, paid your dues, earned a rest—sorry about that: Uncle Sam needs you—again.

Not in uniform this time—behind the front. Inside the ranks of the veterans' organizations you've let go to seed—there's a call for volunteers again.

Recently I heard a call and saw it answered in an unlikely little VFW post in Hendersonville, Tennessee.

While others elsewhere have let the once proud American Legion and Veterans of Foreign Wars fall into disrepute . . . while some places, overweight and underinspired, you left your Post . . . or, worse, you let your Post become known for booze, gambling, bunny-hopping and stag movies . . .

I saw Hendersonville's Post Number 9851 in a shining new building with no bar, a building they gladly share with any

Civic Club, a building they make available as a polling place at election time.

Hendersonville's VFW sponsors Boy Scouts. Christmas time Post 9851 repairs toys and delivers them—along with fruit and candy and food and clothing.

This is the old VFW with a new look.

Once a month, family night. Every family brings a basket of food and all the children.

Periodically the Post imports speakers for patriotic celebrations. Constantly the Post conscientiously recruits new members. For a Veterans' organization without "numbers" is voiceless in Washington. Lawmakers understand only the language of "numbers." Yet despite perpetuated regimentation, more historically important veterans' organizations are dwindling in numbers and importance.

Of course, the Hendersonville VFW Post is not the only VFW or Legion Post devoting itself to civic service and good works, but this one is a worthy example.

Stimulating citizen participation in politics, helping school-agers understand what our ism cost and what it's worth, Post 9851 is adding new glory to Old Glory.

A vast organization with one publicized indiscretion, can get a bad name; it takes tedious years to earn, and constant effort to keep a good one.

I would hope this one Post might inspire a thousand others to get going again, to get the membership off its dead end and back into the front lines of the long neglected home front.

You who knew being an American was worth dying for—know now it's worth working for. Shoulder arms again, Soldier. America has never more desperately needed to be reinspired. I saw a city come to attention to salute a handful. A thousand cities, similarly inspired, will!

YESTERDAY'S MANSIONS INSPIRED AMBITION

Missoula, Montana was a garden spot when Angel and I honeymooned there. Astraddle a sparkling mountain stream, snuggled in a protected valley, with just enough culture imported by the State University and anything you really needed for sale at Missoula Mercantile.

And, for a poor boy, there was the handsome Greenough mansion for inspiration.

Mr. Greenough, a hard working, self-made, successful lumberman, built this handsome 22 room house with its six baths and marble fixtures and several fireplaces and crystal chandeliers as a monument to his success and as a reward for the family which had suffered with him through the long, lean years.

To me, in those very modest years of early marriage, the great Greenough mansion of tamarack wood with a ballroom on its third floor was tangible evidence that Horatio Alger lives on.

Another young man of Missoula, Art Mosby, shared my admiration of that house and was similarly inspired by it.

The Greenoughs eventually moved on to Spokane. The Harveys moved on to seek their fortune elsewhere. Art Mosby stayed and, motivated by that mansion, made his own fortune in Missoula.

I watched, fascinated, from a distance as my long ago friend worked for and then owned the radio station in Missoula, then other radio and TV stations, then real estate.

Eventually, perhaps inevitably, that mansion was his home.

When they announced the new highway was coming through that property, the city was stunned—Mr. Mosby was thunderstruck.

With the casual indifference of bureaucracy it was decreed that the great house with its beautiful stained glass windows and wrought iron fence and wall coverings of velvet and brocade had been condemned by the state and would be destroyed.

I was not particularly surprised subsequently to hear that Art Mosby had bought the house back from the state, offered to move it and to present it to the city as a museum.

But there was no city budget for maintenance and other legal considerations complicated acceptance.

That year, 1965, a fire destroyed much of the mansion's interior. It appeared one of Missoula's oldest landmarks was doomed.

But Mr. Mosby, of stubborn Danish ancestry, refused to give up. He moved the tremendous house as far as the Clark Fork River before the Highway Department refused to allow the overweight house to be moved across the Madison Street bridge.

A less determined man would have abandoned his project. Instead Mr. Mosby conferred with experts—divided the huge structure into three pieces—and thus got it across the river and onto a prominent hilltop southeast of town.

There all Missoula, looking up, can see the mansion, reassembled and restored to its former splendor.

Now Mr. Mosby has opened the old mansion to tours by

visitors. Especially he encourages visits by schoolchildren and young marrieds, hopeful the grand house may mean to them something of what it meant to him, that it might inspire them as it did him . . . not to resent those who have more, but to emulate, imitate and out-do them if we can.

COMMUNISTS ARE JUST ONE PROBLEM

They're slurringly called "professional anti-communists" if that's all they know to talk about. That's a shame. The communist conspiracy worldwide is a very real conspiracy. Home-grown communists are doing their worst to disrupt our society and our economy. They are a very real menace.

But what the more myopic crusaders refuse to recognize is that every communist in the world could drop dead at ten o'clock tomorrow morning and we'd still have most of our problems.

We'd still have almost eight million Americans on welfare. We'd still have bad women shacking up with worthless men because our government pays them with your money for producing illegitimate babies. We'd still be fighting winless wars against other isms. Our streets and our parks would still be unsafe for the people who pay for them.

So just being "against communism" is not enough.

The men generally recognized as the assassins of both President Kennedy and Senator Kennedy embraced, espoused and endorsed communism. Oswald was a Marxist who had rejected the United States and sought asylum in Russia. Sirhan Sirhan was a devoted disciple of the communist ideology.

Hopefully, in the deeds of these men more Americans will be able to recognize the bitter fruits of their Godless religion.

But let's not repeat at home our grotesque blunder in Vietnam where we assumed that aggressive communists were our only problem. They were not. *Our larger problem over there has been our allies.*

Being "against communism," over there or over here, is not enough; we must be "for" something. What we are "for" must be worthy of our dedication.

Hitler and Mussolini were "against communism," but what they were "for" was perhaps worse.

So while it is well and good to remain alert to the party-line Reds in our country, let's be careful that we don't vote ourselves into some other brand of Super State.

There are politicians who run for public office who are not communists, but who nonetheless insist that Big Government is more competent than we, the people. If we continue to vote for more and more big government, what difference does it make whether that government has direct ties with Moscow or Peking?

A dictatorship, by any name, is a national jail.

J. Edgar Hoover writes, "The danger of indiscriminately alleging that someone is a communist, merely because his views on a particular issue happened to parallel the official party position, is obvious. The confusion which is thereby created helps the communists by diffusing the forces of their opponents. Unfortunately, there are those who make the very mistake the communists themselves are so careful to avoid. These individuals concentrate on the negative rather than on the positive. They are merely against communism without being for any positive measure . . ."

Let's listen carefully to what our representatives are "for."

NO MORE DIRT CHEAP

The United States generally and our own underdeveloped areas particularly are caught up in a land boom like nothing our country has seen since the localized Florida promotions of the twenties.

Purposely, so that these words cannot be construed as promoting any specific properties or areas, they are couched in generalities not necessarily applicable everywhere. But almost.

Dr. Tyrus Timm, head of the Department of Agricultural Economics at Texas A & M, says,

"Any land any place in the path of progress is high; none of it is too high!"

This sweeping generality is based on several sound assumptions:

1. Dollars will continue to diminish in value.
2. Industrial expansion will continue.
3. Population will continue to pyramid.
4. Interest rates, however high, are "deductible."
5. Taxes, however high, are "deductible."
6. New Highways enhance values of land heretofore remote, now accessible.

Thus raw land, historically a good hedge against inflation, is now more than ever sought as a sound investment by industry and individuals.

International Paper Company, tree planting, has held vast

63

acreages of fifty-cent land for generations. Now that land is in such demand for planting houses and suburban businesses and industries that the Company is divesting itself of these valuable holdings and buying cheaper land in Canada's bush for growing pulpwood.

Interstate Highways have created a whole new farmland market for motels, service stations, restaurants.

Four million acres of farmland were converted last year to suburban developments, airports, highways, recreational facilities.

Farmers, depressed as the prices for their farm products have been recent years, nonetheless have realized an 8% per year appreciation on their land.

Any "gold rush" attracts pirates, promotors, con men. Yet, so fat is the bull market in land that some promoters are discovering the comparatively worthless lots and acreages they peddled to "pigeons" are being resold for a profit.

Fortunes are accumulated by traders avoiding taxes on transactions by swapping "property in kind" on the perimeters of expanding cities.

Holding land for investment and holding land for sale are two different things in the eyes of the tax man. The dealer in real estate is taxed at regular rates. The man who invests in raw land and, after six months or more, sells it, unimproved, for a profit, benefits from the maximum capital gains tax of 25%.

This incentive has spurred investment in land in many arid non-farm areas where oil and minerals have played out.

Probably, if land values were as readily readable as the stock market, their prices would fluctuate day by day. By any measure, nonetheless, the market in raw land has been a rising market for thirty years and a roaring bull market for the past five.

THE SOUTH HAS RISEN AGAIN

Southern cities and towns have run so hard to catch up that most are now out front!

The excitement in Atlanta and Huntsville and Jackson and thereabouts is more than a gold rush; they are now excelling academically and artistically, too.

Historically our nation's cultural centers were in the eastern population concentrations. New York had opera, Dodge City had Calamity Jane. Philadelphia had the Philharmonic Orchestra, Dallas had Bob Wills and his Texas Playboys.

Not any more.

Once the hard-handed, hairy-chested cattle and oil men had accomplished their financial security they sought social acceptance. They concentrated on importing and then creating educational and cultural opportunities for themselves and their children. They applied themselves to this objective with such diligence and determination that now, more often than not, such opportunities are available to and enjoyed by a greater percentage of provincial Americans.

Meanwhile, in the big eastern cities, stagnation precludes cultural decay.

Now Dallas has the Symphony and Manhattan has the Monkees.

Of course this is not meant to imply that the art forms are no longer available—or even that they are phasing out—in the big, old cities.

But, coming from behind, hinterland America is moving ahead. Provincial Americans, determined not to be outdone, are outdoing!

Recently I attended a convention of oilmen in LaFayette, Louisiana in a magnificently—but artistically and tastefully— decorated ballroom. French delicacies were served on gold table service.

In the way-out-west, also, this coming from behind is becoming apparent. In remote Gallup, New Mexico local Jaycees hosted hundreds by candlelight for such a gourmet meal as I have never seen outside the Spanish embassy.

Private country clubs, last bastion of social exclusivity in older cities, are strangled by tradition, choked by rising property taxes, stifled by ancient, unfunctional architecture.

Private country clubs of incomparable elegance now comprise the multiple social centrifuge of Houston, Phoenix, Greensboro and hundreds of less populous cities.

Further, it has been my observation that if they have available less theatre and fewer concerts, nonetheless they enjoy those opportunities more frequently than do we for whom they are available every day.

Admittedly, one factor accelerating progress in our own "underdeveloped" areas is the fact that there is more growing room.

Still that does not explain all of it. The middle-size town of Anniston, Alabama is clearing sixty mid-town acres to create our nation's first educational "supermarket," a vast complex of modern classrooms, kindergarten through junior college.

This renaissance which started with a "we'll show you" attitude is still gaining momentum. The South has risen again! If they don't get so fat they get lazy, their skyscrapers will put us all in the shade.

SNOW IS COLD

Mine are always the first footprints in the new snow, the first tire tracks on the streets of our Chicago suburb at five in the morning.

Reflected light illumines even that dark hour.

It is so beautiful.

Snow appears so pure, so innocent—is so treacherous.

Falls so softly—packs so hard.

Snow, negligee of white lace hiding the nakedness of winter branches—heavier and heavier until under the sheer weight of all the loveliness, they break . . . and fall.

Snow . . . white, sugar-coated blanket of deceit . . . luring the unsuspecting with its gentle promise . . .

Then sending them sprawling.

Snow is cold.

Enticing even little children to come out and play . . . then sending them home from fairyland wet and sniffling.

Yet, I love it. With a strange, unrequited love I am irresistibly attracted to this calculating mistress of the streets. A hundred ways, a thousand times she has tried to destroy that love. Demanding the tedious attention of shovel, broom and woodlot.

Snow is cold.

Once I thought if we could live and work and play together it would be different. That understanding would make her kind. And so I learned with skiis to walk with her to the mountaintops where she is most at home. To caress the steep incline and through the blur of whirling flakes . . . down, down the fluffy slopes to glide . . .

But the fluff was only there to hide—the rocks.

Snow is cold.

Clings to my wings if I threaten to fly away from her.

Conspires to stain her own spotlessness with blood. Yet I know she would calmly conceal even that stain with a magic sifting of herself and go on her merry way as if nothing had happened.

Only in the city's sidestreets do I sometimes catch a glimpse of her soiled . . . by her own sordid misadventures. But I can never let myself remember her like that.

She has stalled my car in driveway drifts. Or, with sadistic glee, has hurled it and me uncontrolled against curbside or tree. Yet from each rebuff I pick myself up . . . swear vengeance . . . abandon this cruel courtship . . . retire to the warm fire that helps me to forget her loveliness.

Yet each time we are apart it's the same.

I can't wait to see her again.

BONNET WITH A CAPITAL "B"

Where would you find two women who would want to wear identical Easter Bonnets? In 1880 five women did. Today more than a million women do.

No feathers, lace and frippery, this chapeau. It must be austere black—but sturdy enough to protect the wearer from a flying brickbat.

For its designer was Catherine Booth. And this Bonnet, essentially unaltered to this day, is regulation apparel for the lady officers of the Salvation Army.

The sturdy Bonnet is made of Milan straw and imported silk. Its price, though small compared to high fashion contemporary hats, is nonetheless considerable for a Salvation Army Cadet.

Yet to the novice that first Bonnet is worth saving for—worth sacrificing for—for it is symbolic of her "coming of age," spiritually. And for a Cadet, Grandmother's Bonnet is the most treasured heirloom imaginable.

In the beginning, the protective Bonnet had a wider coal-scuttle brim. That has been modified. That is, the brim became less wide as the need for protection diminished.

The gap in the back of the Bonnet is to allow for the Cadet's long hair. During the interim between then and now, when hair styles were short, the Cadet in full formal dress was expected to wear a bun of artificial hair to complete her ensemble.

So durable is the traditional Bonnet, and so precious a symbol, that many more than half a century old are still being worn.

And however the Bonnet may have been stoned, scorned or ridiculed, it is trusted all over the world.

An anxious mother, sending a small son off on his first train trip in Illinois, sighted a Bonnet among the departing passengers. "Would the Bonnet please look after Junior?" It would.

The mother, thus reassured and relieved, trustfully waved a cheerful goodbye to her son—and the Bonnet.

Foreigners, lost, confused and frightened on a New York street, anxiously eyeing passers-by for a friendly face, suddenly delight to recognize this world symbol of compassion and assistance—The Bonnet.

People in trouble anywhere in the world gravitate toward the Bonnet.

The Bonnet has been cursed and crowned with thorns and stained with blood but it has never been disgraced. Indicative of the respect it has earned, this hat has no nickname, either within the Army or without. It is the "Bonnet"—and it's spelled with a Capital "B."

It is inevitable in an era of compromise, accommodation and subversion that some would modify the Salvation Army uniform, a few would abandon it.

May this Easter Bonnet for any season remain as is forever. When I awaken on resurrection morning the first thing I'm going to look for is a Bonnet. If I see that, I'll know I'm in the right place.

FOR WHOM THE BELL TOLLS

Not everything the world calls progress is. This is: In one generation our nation's most deplorable discrimination has been dissolved.

You can remember when we locked up "nuts" in the "crazy house."

Gradually we learned more about mental derangement, yet confined "insane" people to the "asylum."

Now we know there is a wide spectrum of mental and emotional illnesses ranging from your own depression at the tired end of a busy day to the pathologically violent. A whole new vocabulary is applicable as the mentally ill emerge from hopelessness to hope, from unemployable to employed, as they step out of the dark and into the light.

Much of the credit for accelerating this evolution goes to the National Mental Health Association.

This is an organization of concerned individuals. The government applauds it but does not sponsor it. These volunteers, many with a family experience with mental illness, many with family names you would recognize, contribute their time, money and talents to fighting mental illnesses through science, service and social action.

The symbol of this organization is a bell, a huge 300 pound bell of special significance. On ceremonial occasions—as for

71

the annual launching of Mental Health Month—this bell is rung by a statesman or other dignitary, ranging from Presidents through an assortment of distinguished health officials and including at least one prominent baseball player.

I'd like to tell you more about that bell and that ballplayer against this background: One out of every two hospital beds in the United States is occupied by a mental patient. Further, though one in 20 of us is in a mental hospital, one in 10 should be.

Fortunately, most of those whom we formerly locked away in the attic or the snake pit do respond to modern therapy. Improved drug therapy and applied psychiatry have multiplied the discharge rate of our mental hospitals. Between 70% and 85% of the patients admitted with psychoses are now being released within months, often within weeks! The Mental Health Association's dedicated volunteers finance improved facilities, seek to upgrade conditions in mental hospitals, to improve treatment, to facilitate rehabilitation. But Brewer Grant, Chicago area MHA executive, believes the most significant single accomplishment has been the changed vocabulary. We're talking about the things we used to whisper about. Indeed, we are proclaiming progress on this vital warfront with the ear-splitting thunder of a giant bell.

McShane Foundry in Baltimore emptied a chamber of horrors to gather the metal which was melted and poured into the making of that symbolic bell. For the metal—gathered from all across our nation—was made up of chains, shackles, leg irons and the torturous host of barbarous restraints which characterized our historic, cruel confinement of the mentally ill.

One of that great bell's grandest hours was one recent day in Fenway Park, Boston.

Jimmy Piersall, Red Sox outfielder, had just recovered from

two years of mental illness. He was back in the lineup and playing better than ever.

When Piersall banged the clapper against the side of that symbolic bell, he knew those for whom that bell tolls, he knew the message it proclaimed: There is hope. There is progress. And for more every day there is victory.

WHO'LL HAVE THE LAST LAUGH?

Jokes travel our nation these days at the speed of light. Often the same joke has a different target in each state.

I hear jokes told on the Italians in New York, on the Polish in Chicago, on the Aggies in Texas. The same jokes. Only the names have been changed to make fun of some local whipping boy.

In Montana Montanans tell stories about North Dakotans: "The power failed and it took the North Dakotan two hours to figure out how to get off the stalled escalator."

North Dakotans tell the same stories on Norwegians: "He broke his shoulder raking leaves; he fell out of the tree!"

Norwegians tell the same stories another way: "Did you hear about the Canadian who went ice fishing? He came home with fifty pounds of ice."

English-speaking Canadians will advise: "Never hire a Frenchman elevator operator; he can't remember the route."

Whom do they impale on their barbed jests in upper Michigan?

"It takes three Finns to change a light bulb; one to hold the bulb and two to turn the ladder."

Where upper Michigan laughs at the expense of Finns, the Detroit area makes fun of the frugality of Hollanders: "The Grand Canyon was dug by a Hollander looking for a penny."

Whom do they baste with tears of laughter in Nebraska? If you live south of Omaha you pick on the Polish (The Polock). North of Omaha the butt of the same jokes is the Bohemian (The Bohunk).

"He equipped his car with snow tires but when he went out the next morning they'd melted."

Pennsylvanians joke about "The Dutch," but with an undertone of respect: "Lancaster Amishman explaining his damaged watch to the jeweler, 'I only dropped it once and I picked it up real quick.'"

When an Ohioan tells a tall tale about a West Virginian he may be less kind: "The best place to hide money from a hillbilly is under the soap."

In southern Indiana they contemplate "the largest zoo in the world; we'll fence in Kentucky."

These little wars go on all over the world.

In Hawaii, it's the Portuguese who never win: "He can't make any more ice cubes; he lost the recipe."

In upper New York State it's the "dumb Swede" who never gets a coffee break because "it would take too much time to retrain him afterward."

In southern New York the butt of the same joke may be Italian or Jewish or "the guy from Brooklyn who smelled good on only one side; he didn't know where to buy any Left Guard."

One of the wonderful things about our melting pot nation is that all Americans are "mostly something else."

Recently, Negroes have been made hyper-sensitive about Negro jokes, but significantly Negro-white relations have not been improved by this blackout.

Other American minorities suffer sometimes hurtful humor philosophically. They figure you always find the most clubs under the tree with the best apples on it.

HANDCUFFS ON THE WRONG HANDS

I am your policeman. I feel compelled to warn you that there is a man lurking across the street from your home. Part the curtains. Look. Over there by the curbside tree. In a car or afoot he has been passing your house at least twice a day recently.

I know who he is! I do not know what he's up to. Perhaps he is determining what hours the house is empty or what time your daughter is there alone.

The man observing you from the shadows is well known to us policemen.

His name is Murk. Let me tell you about Murk.

He did time in Angola for rape, in Joliet for armed robbery. He's been arrested for breaking-and-entering, mugging, pandering. Twenty-four times in thirteen years. Convicted six times. The one time he went up for ten he was back in two.

Judging from his m.o., Murk is casing your place for burglary. Or as I say, he could be more interested in your daughter. Crimes of passion are more prevalent in summertime.

You can go to the telephone and call us—the police—if you like—but there is nothing we can do.

We had Murk in last week when the Williams' house was burglarized and the week before when that schoolgirl was waylaid under the viaduct. He laughed at us.

Years ago we'd have taken Murk off to the police station, told him we had evidence, demanded an alibi for the time of the crime and booked him. Not any more.

Now the Supreme Court says if we arrest Murk on "suspicion," we must immediately and in front of witnesses advise him:

1. You don't have to say anything.
2. If you do say anything, it can and will be used as evidence against you in a court of law.
3. If you do not have a lawyer, the State will provide one.
4. You do not have to talk until your lawyer gets here.

We policemen carry a little card with all this rigamarole written out to be sure we say it right. Murk has it memorized.

So he sits there and smirks until we let him go.

Or, if we do call a lawyer for him, the lawyer smirks: "You mean no witnesses?"

So we have to let him go anyway.

That, dear citizen, is why there is a dangerous man watching your home from across the street.

If it is any comfort to you, Murk has not murdered anybody —yet.

But other recent Supreme Court rulings on the selection of juries have all but abolished the death sentence, so he might.

Chief Justice John C. Bell, Jr. of the Pennsylvania Supreme Court said, "Recent Supreme Court decisions which shackle police and lower courts have jeopardized the future welfare of the United States. Respect for law and lawmen is vanishing. It is now almost impossible for the policeman to protect you from crime and criminals."

The Fraternal Order of Police is trying to counter-attack, is seeking fifty million signatures on a petition to force nullification of recent Supreme Court rulings.

Until some such effort is successful, there is nothing we can do about Murk.

The High Court has handcuffed the wrong hands.

GUN CONTROL NO CRIME
DETERRENT

Frightened Americans who think we, the people, cannot be trusted with guns . . . and others who want us disarmed and helpless for other reasons . . . failed to get all the gun controls they wanted from Congress. Now they are trying, state by state, to restrict the sale of guns and to force the registration of gun owners.

Many states now require registration of gun owners. Taxation comes next. Then, history says, confiscation comes last.

The four states which have the strongest gun laws are New Jersey, New York, Massachusetts and West Virginia.

The four states which have the least gun controls are Kansas, Kentucky, Minnesota and Vermont.

The *states with the least gun controls have a lower murder rate* than those states with the toughest gun controls: 3.9 per 100,000 population compared to 4.1 per 100,000 in the strict states.

For those who sincerely believe that the answer to crime is to outlaw guns, let's consider New Jersey.

The state of New Jersey was the first in our nation to place severe restrictions on firearms of all kinds. With few exceptions, New Jersey residents are required by law to obtain police-issued permits—after being fingerprinted—before they can carry rifles, shotguns or handguns.

Since that law became effective in 1966, *crime in New Jersey has increased.*

Formerly New Jersey had less armed robbery and killing than the national average; now it has more than the national average. New Jersey now has a higher crime rate than 39 other states.

Now may I introduce a lawbreaking criminal who directed a profitable flow of underworld gun traffic between Chicago and Detroit for two years before he got caught. Fred Green, now in prison, says "the hottest commodity on the underworld market is stolen *registered* guns."

Green says, "If I can pull a job and leave behind a stolen .45, and if the registered owner of that gun cannot prove where he was at that time, nobody will be looking for me."

Green says, "National gun control? Knowing what we are willing to do to get guns, these guys must be kidding! Did they keep us from getting booze during prohibition?"

Most Americans who do not possess guns are unconcerned about registration, licensing fees, etc. They should be concerned. In Philadelphia the permit required for a gun purchase costs the purchaser only one dollar. But the paperwork to administer this monumental bookkeeping operation costs each taxpayer fifteen dollars per gun!

Yearly, this effort is costing Philadelphia taxpayers approximately ten million dollars. That much money would hire a thousand additional policemen.

And significantly, Philadelphia's assistant district attorney in charge of prosecuting homicide cases, said, "This panic legislation resulting from the assassination of President Kennedy has had no effect whatever on the homicide rate in our city."

The defense rests.

NATION ON THE NEEDLE

Welfare is a habit forming and potentially deadly narcotic and must be so labelled.

During the depression of the thirties, FDR employed emergency measures to meet that emergency.

He closed banks, created WPA jobs for the jobless, established soup kitchens to feed the hungry and otherwise softened the blow, cushioned the shock, narcoticized the hurt.

When our sick economy got well, banks were reopened, the "madework" was discontinued. But politicians had found the welfare handout such attractive vote bait that the voter was given additional and increasing doses of this narcotic. Inevitably, we were addicted—helplessly "hooked."

In treating physical ills, the doctors are always extremely careful to phase out the dosage of any pain-killing drug as promptly as possible to prevent the patient from becoming addicted.

The welfare narcotic—though similarly habit forming and potentially fatal—was continued. Politicians learned that they could get the voter to vote any way they wanted him to vote if only they would promise to perpetuate the soothing, comforting, tranquilizing jabs from that welfare needle.

Today one in twenty-five Americans is on that "dope" and the number of "addicts" is increasing twice as fast as our population is increasing.

Recently the House half of Congress heard from Mrs. Sadie Willis of East Liverpool. She said, "Any human who gets something for nothing loses his pride; there's always work to be done and the government should simply tell the loafer— you don't work, you don't eat!"

Mrs. Sadie Willis, a Negro, was applauded from the gallery and from the floor.

But Congress went right ahead and voted to perpetuate the gigantic federal welfare program.

It's now so desperately difficult to get household help in most American cities and towns that the Department of Labor is encouraging housemaids to come from overseas to fill these jobs . . . while 7,800,000 Americans remain on welfare.

In Warren, Pennsylvania welfare recipient William Karns asked the county surplus food director for "more raisins to make wine." He was told the limit is one box for a family of two. He'll have to save up.

In Charlotte, North Carolina a woman said her welfare check was so insufficient she was reduced to shoplifting for food. The Judge suggested, instead, that she sell her Cadillac. People on New York City's welfare rolls are allowed to spend their relief checks on state lottery tickets.

Isolated as these ludicrous instances are, they are symtomatic of the desperate degree to which so many Americans are already hooked. Historically, freeloading has been fatal.

What politician will have the courage to prescribe the painful, however necessary, withdrawal?

IF EVERY BLACK TURNED WHITE TONIGHT

If every black turned white tonight, tomorrow morning we would find most of our problems unresolved.

Statistically, we would have less crime—but we would still have much too much. The percentage of whites committing crimes is about five times greater than the white population increase.

We would still have unemployment in the midst of plentiful jobs, because 40% of the unemployed are white.

We would still have mothers bearing illegitimate children to make themselves eligible for increasing welfare handouts.

We would still have unwon wars overseas and resultant domestic restiveness.

Many Americans have been allowing themselves to adopt the ancient scapegoat concept, imagining that we can absolve ourselves of our own sins by blaming everything on the blacks. We can't.

Indeed, the black-white relationship in the United States, in perspective, amounts to a very commendable amalgamation.

Historically, many of the world's diverse cultures have not been able to pull so close together in 2,000 years as our black-white cultures have in 200 years.

Britain, for all her centuries of involvement with Africans and Asiatics, is less close to them than we Americans are to one another.

That we have domestic black-white strife involving fractions of our black-white populations should not be nearly so surprising as the larger fact that we have come so far so fast in providing equality of opportunity and mutual social acceptance.

I do not intend to try to defend the so-called black "militants."

It is too obvious that many of them have a chip on their shoulders, resenting their own blackness—and that they use blackness as a catalyst for mobilizing resentment, restiveness and rebellion.

They are as wrong to blame all their troubles on their color as we are to blame all our troubles on them.

That's why I say every black could turn white tonight and tomorrow morning we would still have legions of lazy Americans demanding more for working less.

We would still have large segments of our college and university populations going to "pot."

We would still have young Americans burning our flag because they resent the maladministration of some of our foreign affairs and foolishly blame our ism.

We would still have rebellious youths growing long hair and wearing dirty clothes in rebellion against a generation of parents who drink and say "don't" and smoke and say "don't" and who denounce misusing sex while they do.

If every black should turn white tonight, we'd still have too many hungry and unenlightened Mexicans, Indians and shantytown whites.

We'd still have public nudity, lurid movies and putrid magazines feeding carnal appetites of corruptible Caucasians.

So most of what ails us is not so simply dismissed as a matter of black and white.

If every black turned white tonight, tomorrow morning we would still have most of our problems . . .

And so would they!

TO MY SON

Dear Son:

Whatever happened to the past fifteen years? Before I got a chance to talk to you about the birds and bees, you could tell me—and in Latin.

Up to here you've probably taught mother and me more than we've taught you.

But just once, before you grow too completely away from us, I'd like you to look at some notes which I've written to myself over the years.

You'll do what your own ideals demand and seek what your own heart desires, regardless, but if your intelligence could somehow pick up where Dad's knowledge leaves off, it would spare you some skinned shins. Some of them, not all of them.

So that's the first entry in my notebook, and the last one: Get up when you fall down.

We all fall down. But the thing that separates the men from the boys is that a man gets up when he falls down.

Bear down on your school work, not just because the world needs you—but because you're going to need it. If you excel in what you do, you'll have to eat less crow; it's as simple as that.

I suggest you don't load up your closet with skeletons. Every time you make an unerasable mistake, you'll have to carry that extra load the whole distance. This goes for the Commie causes which might tempt your heart, the con game that might get you an indelible police record, the girl you might disgrace, the disease you go looking for and the carelessness which costs a limb or a life. Think overtime trying to anticipate and avoid unerasable mistakes.

Smile a lot. Son, there are only two ways you can pay your membership dues in the human race. You owe enthusiasm to your employer and pleasantness to your associates.

There are no two qualities of character which will reward you, personally, materially and otherwise, more than those two—enthusiasm and pleasantness.

For goodness sake, find a work that interests you and stick with it. I said work "that interests you." That is enough to ask. No job is all fun or all easy or even all pleasant, but if your job isn't interesting you're going to hoe a long, hard row.

Son, time is going to mellow you eventually whether you like it or not, but there'll be less wear and tear on you if you can roll with it. And you'll have your hair longer. Maybe your teeth, too.

You have your Dad's stubborn convictions about certain things. That's all right. I'm glad you do. But don't ever deny the other fellow's rights to have his convictions, too.

What I'm saying is that time is going to teach you a certain patience, even with impatience, a degree of tolerance, even for intolerance.

I hope you don't drink or smoke much, because life has a way of overcharging a fellow for overindulgence.

I hope you don't swear much. Any durn fool can swear.

And when the world looks lopsided, remember that you, personally, are being sized up for a more symmetrical place.

If you can—measure up.

LET'S LEARN FROM VIETNAM

Mistakes are no disgrace if we profit from them. In the laboratory we are perfectly willing to accept and admit the failure of a research project because each has taught us something. If nothing else, from disappointment scientists learn *what will not work*.

Similarly, in a military campaign we probe for enemy weaknesses and with no apology for temporary reverses. Losing yesterday's battles teaches us improved strategy for tomorrow's. A strategic retreat can defeat a Napoleon.

While we have learned to accept reversals in the laboratory and on the battlefield, we somehow imagine that a diplomatic blunder is a disgrace. Time and again our diplomats, seeking to cover up mistakes, have compounded them.

Vietnam is a dead end for American diplomacy.

We goofed. We meddled where we should have not. Seeking to rescue an unworthy Saigon government, we alienated the southeast Asians we had hoped to encourage.

It is conceded now that the United States will not make this mistake again.

Though we have treaties with forty-one other nations similar to the one which involved us in Vietnam, our State Department and our Pentagon have had enough.

Though we are willing to concede that Vietnam must not

happen again, our leaders are yet unwilling to confess the failure of this "mission impossible."

In Paris we offer to get out of Vietnam and leave behind all the bases we built there and we have promised to help reconstruct what we damaged in North and South Vietnam and eventually it is a virtual certainty that one government will unify North and South and it will not be particularly friendly to us.

Yet—acknowledging all this—that we were wrong—that we failed—that we want out—that we will get out—

Still we delay that inescapable eventuality by proclaiming, "We are not going to turn the United States into a third-rate power by bugging out!"

We lacked the stomach for an all-out military war when it might have been both meaningful and decisive. Now we will withdraw and salvage nothing.

We must stop deluding ourselves with heroic utterances which are totally lacking in meaning.

We "bugged out" of Cuba without being reduced to a third-rate power.

Indeed, those Americans so anxious about which way southeast Asia's dominoes might fall appear blind to the more imminent menace in Latin America.

Hopefully, however, we learned something from our under-extension at the Bay of Pigs.

Hopefully we will learn from our over-extension in Vietnam.

If we learn what not to do next time, then we may well benefit more from defeat than from victory.

THE FALSE PROPHETS

Oregon's Wayne Morse, while he was Senator, said, "Bombing North Vietnam will start World War Three." He made that dogmatic and dire prediction before 900 students at Fairleigh Dickinson University in Teaneck, New Jersey April 28, 1966.

For this and similarly undiscerning utterances his own party almost dumped him in his own state in 1968. He did lose the election.

Predictions are fun in a carnival sideshow but can be fatal for professional politicians.

Often, reaching for a headline, the orator will presume to predict the future.

Unfortunately, many Americans still accept "they say" guesstimates as gospel. "It's going to happen," the naive insist, "I read it in the paper!"

How many American investors ran scared because Yale economist James Tobin, in February of 1967, predicted an immediate recession?

Eliot Janeway, in 1966, said, "The stock market has only begun to retreat; in 1967 it will be a shambles!"

Similarly, University of Chicago Professor, Milton Friedman, February 13, 1967, predicted recession that year.

They were all wrong.

So were the hundreds of Danes who crawled into caves

Christmas Eve 1967 because their cult leader, Knud Weiking, had seen "a vision that there will be an atomic war before midnight."

Many Americans assume because Ohio's Cyrus Eaton is so often entertained and applauded by Moscow that he has an "in" with the Russians. His utterances are given attention all out of proportion to their credibility. As when he said May 25, 1965, "Russia is ready to enter the Vietnam war; unless something occurs in the next month mankind is doomed."

It wasn't.

Some of these self-appointed modern wise men are unduly optimistic. Atomic Energy Chairman Dr. Glenn Seaborg, October 19, 1964, was confident, "Red China is five years away from the capability of a thermo-nuclear reaction."

They had it *the next year.*

Defense Secretary McNamara told Lyndon Johnson in November of 1966 that "draft calls may be cut in half next year." They were increased, instead.

Newsweek Magazine, November 30, 1964 said, "J. Edgar Hoover is on his way out as FBI Director." He wasn't, hopefully still isn't.

London Times said, November 27, 1964, "The United States will go to war with Red China by the end of the year or soon thereafter."

False.

Florida's Senator George A. Smathers, September 12, 1964, predicted the "downfall of Cuban Premier Castro will come in 1965."

It didn't.

British Foolosopher, Bertrand Russell, who knows everything about everything, announced February 23, 1959, "I am going to die June 1, 1962."

He hasn't yet.

Playwright Tennessee Williams gave the human race "ten more years of existence" eleven years ago.

One of our nation's most respected news magazines in May 1968 published articles three weeks apart affirming that "the dollar is doomed" and "the dollar is the world's strongest currency and getting stronger."

What "they say" may be interesting. Just don't bet on it.

IS ONE WIFE NOT ENOUGH?

Printed and widely reprinted in the nation's press was a recent statement by a New York psychologist, Dr. Albert Ellis: "Adultery may be good for you."

This is not the first time this theoretical psychologist has focused attention on himself with a sensational public utterance, but this one was seized upon, hashed and rehashed by frequently cynical newshawks, until an individual's outlandish theory is being repronounced with such pomposity that it is assuming an unwarranted degree of authenticity.

Dr. Ellis says people are not truly monogamous, that romantic love is not durable, that it never lasts more than three to five years if the participants are under the same roof.

So, he concludes, "adultery can be a healthy way of preventing a marriage from disintegrating."

When a man has a "Reverend" or an "Honorable" or a "Doctor" prefixing his name, his words are likely to receive an endowment of credulity which they may not rightly deserve.

I know of one chap taking up a collection nationwide in support of a kookie cult who is, in fact, a "doctor" and who was, in fact, a "professor." Yet he has a credibility gap as wide as his ears.

Today's front page is a mirror of what happens when we ignore basic moral law. Whether you believe the commandments are sacred, it is the consensus of scholars that they are the best available blueprint for an orderly existence. If the Bible did not promise life hereafter it would still be the best rule book for a good life here.

The idea Dr. Ellis enunciates is not original with him. Sigmund Freud decided, before Dr. Ellis was born, that sex repression was bad for you, that these animal urges should be released—however indiscriminately.

He lived to repent and retract many of his conclusions.

Similarly, Russia's more recent attempt at encouraging sexual permissiveness bore bitter fruit, has been rescinded.

Dr. Ellis, an instant expert on how to keep marriages from disintegrating, has himself been married twice.

If one day he's had a few more wives and gets to the end of the road without any he may want to correct himself.

These days we are all living on the steep slopes of a rumbling volcano. The next time my phone rings it may be World War Three. It is understandable if such a precarious perch makes some people faint and others dizzy.

If there is sometimes sex in suburbia, there is sometimes homicide, too. Yet it is hardly to the best interests of society to advocate an open season.

Today's assortment of unkempt and frequently diseased beatnik types, now on a "doctor's prescription" can parade their dirtiness while advocating extra-marital sex or free love or whatever.

But they are a shabby showcase for what he and they are peddling.

ONE PLUS ONE EQUALS ELEVEN

Homer McKee, the Hoosier philosopher, liked to refer to a compatible man-woman relationship as a multiplication of itself.

"One and one adds up to more than two when you are dealing with the human equation. Stand the one and one side by side and they equal eleven."

The most monumental example in contemporary history is the relationship between Sir Winston Churchill and his "Clemmie" which profited the world.

The splendid biography, "My Darling Clementine," details much of the inter-reliance which was his and hers.

"And then I was married," wrote Sir Winston, "and lived happily ever after."

The degree to which they complimented one another is inseparable from the record of his accomplishments.

Similarly, the star of Napoleon was on the ascendancy throughout his marriage to Josephine. Until their divorce in 1807, he could do nothing wrong. From then on, it seemed, he could do nothing right.

Spanish resistance, Russian intransigence, Germanic rebellion—history blames these for his demise and destruction.

But whatever else contributed, when Bonaparte ran out on Josephine he ran out of luck.

How dramatic the contrast, within our own memory, between the Churchills on one hand and the Hitlers and Mussolinis on the other.

Twenty-some years ago Mussolini and his mistress tried to slink out of Italy, were caught on Lake Como, and killed. The next day the bodies of Mussolini and Claretta Petacci were trucked into Milan, mauled by angry crowds, then hanged by the heels in front of a gas station.

About that same time, Hitler put a pistol in his mouth and his mistress, Eva Braun, put cyanide in hers. Then they were wrapped in rude blankets and burned in a bomb crater.

One-and-one made two graves.

So the man-woman equation Homer McKnee described must be something more than an expedient relationship. It must be endowed with the marriage magic—the inexplicable quality of self magnification.

Then one-and-one, side-by-side, becomes eleven.

There is a conspicuously productive relationship not to be overlooked in our own White House.

The closeness of the Nixons is more than an admirable political image; it is a workable, effective, fruitful union.

So genuinely did former President Johnson subscribe to the "McKee equation" that he established unprecedented protocol for all US Ambassadors. Before going on their assignments, they were to *bring their wives* to the White House.

And President Nixon has emphasized the man-wife combination at such times as the announcing of his cabinet members and at the Inaugural. Even when, later, members of the cabinet took their oaths, it was each wife who, holding the Bible, stood beside her husband.

That was not only wise, it was smart. That way President Nixon gets 11 times each man.

Similarly, prior to any White House appointment of importance, the background and interests of the nominee's wife are considered.

More and more, industry is similarly concerned with this relationship in the selection of top level personnel.

A good marriage does not guarantee success, but it multiplies the odds in its favor.

YOUNG MAN—GO LIVE SOME
PLACE BEAUTIFUL

Generations of small town American youths were attracted by bright lights and economic opportunities to the big cities.

Now the big cities have less to offer than the countryside. Young man, *go live some place beautiful.*

When most of us came home from the Big War we asked ourselves, "What do we want to do?"

When Lance Day came home from that war he asked himself, "Where do I want to live?" He asked the right question.

Lance Day had always liked green mountains, blue sky and fast water. He remembered reading about the Greenbrier in West Virginia, decided he would like to live there.

Who wouldn't? Since stagecoach days that gracious resort had been a retreat for the most affluent and the most discriminating. How dare a young ex GI with no money presume to *live* there!

Lance Day sought and got a job in the lower level haberdashery in the Greenbrier Hotel, soon managed it, then owned it.

Day married, made a down payment on a nearby hillside home, started rearing a family in that beautiful environment. Later he opened a ladies' shop, then a children's shop in the Greenbrier—with wintertime branches in Lake Placid and

96

Sarasota. Perhaps he is less rich in the bank than many of that spa's guests, but he is many ways richer.

By contrast, in Chicago, seven million people are piled on top of one another. The nearest hunting or fishing are at least a state away in Wisconsin or Michigan. The last Chicago golf course is now a hard hour's drive from downtown. Those closer in have been phased out, subdivided.

Chicago's parks and forest preserves, once available for picnicking, hiking, kite-flying, are now mostly hangouts for hooligans. A year ago Chicago had four riding stables; the last of those closed this year.

Even on clear days in the Big City, a pall of industrial weather filters the sun and hides the stars.

Go some place beautiful, young man. With transportation at the speed of sound and communication at the speed of light there is no longer any necessity or any advantage or any reason for most Americans to be cliff dwellers in the concrete canyons of a megalopolis.

There is the magnificent American Northwest, the exciting anything-you-want variety in our Southwest. There are a thousand shangri-las in our Northeast and Southeast all within reach of metropolitan areas and still uncontaminated by them.

Just out of school, just home from war, try the formula Lance Day used for planning his future. Instead of asking yourself, "What do I want to do?" (unless there is some compelling ambition inhibiting your choice) ask yourself, "Where do I want to live?"

Then go there.

Horace Greeley advised young men of his generation to "Go West" while he stayed East and got rich. Paul Harvey says, "Go some place beautiful."

THE OLD CAR

The graceful white coupe in which we had our first date was a Nash Lafayette.

At the memory of some of the confidences it shared and the trysts it sheltered, I blush yet.

When the brash young newsman asked the pretty blonde studying to be a schoolteacher to marry him, the car was hers.

When she said yes it became ours—twenty-five years ago.

It drove us from St. Louis across the United States, then home again from a Honolulu honeymoon.

As ensuing years rolled under her many times recapped tires, the Old Nash became a member of the family. In the days when it was still all uphill, the three of us made the grade together.

As soon as the Harveys could afford Lake Shore Drive in Chicago, the old car got a new coat of paint.

And one day we drove to the hospital, three, and drove home, four.

The sentimental Harveys were not willing to commit their aging friend to the ignominy of an old car graveyard. So, when the old car, its stick shift and running boards outdated and its innards in decay like the one-horse shay, was about to give up the ghost—we drove her one last time down Highway 66.

Huffing and puffing, engine rattling, radiator steaming, I forced her through the gate, into our Ozarks farm, propped her up on concrete blocks in the barn and left her there.

Each new farm hand complained once that she was "in the way." He was answered by icewater silence. Thus the old car, rotting and rusting, haven for mice, moths and barn birds, stayed put.

Recently I arrived on the campus of John Brown University in Siloam Springs, Arkansas for a scheduled speech. I was watching the happy homecoming activities in the crowded quadrangle when suddenly the crowd of people parted . . . and turned eyes-right.

For a moment my eyes were blinded by the bright sunlight.

And then I saw it. Moving through the throng.

Then, above a cacophany of cheers—the honk of a horn I had not heard for many years. Moving through that sunlit sea of people was the ghost of an old, old friend.

John Brown had rescued her from our farm barn, students had refurbished, refinished, repainted, re-upholstered. Bumpers were sparkling chrome again. Smashed lights renewed, hubcaps by now collectors' items, replaced. Every dent was smooth. The gallant old engine was purring as she had on that first night.

A sudden torrent of memories flooded the sunlit scene. The old car was new—and I was young again.

On this twenty-fifth year of our marriage, John Brown University was presenting us with the car in which it all began.

I recall no experience so overwhelming as this. All the memories of sunlit days and moon-drenched nights—of the drive away to war and home again—all the bittersweetness of that montage of memories. Speechless, I climbed in and drove away until I could swallow again.

She has returned to our Ozarks farm. A separate garage has been built for her there.

The old car, like the love it represents, has had many scratches healed, many dents smoothed over. Yet after a quarter century and more it is still shining new.

POLITICIANS EMPLOY GAG WRITERS

Wit is the most effective but the most dangerous of all political weapons.

Churchill mastered its use as few have.

I heard Sir Winston, in Commons and in schoolhouse campaigns, humble adversaries with a rapier phrase sharp enough to make its point felt—yet never quite sharp enough to draw blood.

It was a phrase half way between clever and cruel which once defeated Richard Nixon for the Presidency. The phrase, appearing under his almost-always-unflattering photograph said: "Would you buy a used car from this man?"

That image-destroying joke was coined in 1960 by a professional humor-author, Robert Orben, who was in demand by politicians of both parties for one-line "funnies" with which to spice their campaign oratory.

Orben says it was not his intention to hurt Mr. Nixon. He insists that his widely-published comedy quotes "reflect trends" rather than "create trends."

Review his monthly mailings to clients during the two years prior to the 1964 election and on that barometer the rise and fall of political issues and political candidates is easily traceable.

Marvin Marx was chief writer for Jackie Gleason. President

Kennedy was so impressed with his sense of humor, Marx was employed to submit jokes for Presidential speeches.

You can trace the rise of Goldwater's public acceptance toward nomination time—"Barry's life will be filmed by Nineteenth Century Fox."

And the decline toward election time—"In your heart you know he's right; in your guts you know he's nuts."

Orben says, "There is no better way to assess the impact a candidate is making than by the reaction of audiences to jokes about him." He believes McNamara was laughed out of Washington with such barbed phrases as: "They offered McNamara the job of Baseball Commissioner but he wanted to close second base."

Or, "The man who gave us the Edsel can't be infallible."

Orben believes that "jokes, tailored to attack specific enemies, are the political weapon of the future. As politicians have historically employed speech writers, they now will employ gag-writers. Many already do." Orben does not identify his own clients, for obvious reasons. He does admit that he was on retainer by "a political party" during the 1964 campaign.

Many American statesmen and women have made good use of a personal gift of wit, from Abe Lincoln through Everett Dirkson and including Clare Booth Luce.

Adlai Stevenson "almost" had it, but he overshot the target as consistently as most professional politicians are inclined to undershoot it.

"Orbenisms" have some of the light touch with which Will Rogers helped us smile at topical headlines: "Noah Kennedy is sending out a dove named McCarthy to look for land."

"I'd rather fight than switch! Now if we could only convince the South Vietnamese."

Presently there are 250 comedy writers in show business, another 100 writing jokes for advertising and industry. Orben

102

believes there will be ten times that many grinding out material for politicians within the next two decades.

So the "isn't he clever!" candidate may have earned your praise. More likely he bought it.

MORMON WELFARE WORKS!

Historically in our country charity was the responsibility of the Church.

Admonished by the fifteenth chapter of Deuteronomy that, "Thou shalt open thine hand wide to the poor," our churches saw to the needs of the needy. The Mormon Church still does.

The Apostle Paul further admonished, "He who will not work, let him not eat."

In the Mormon Church a phenomenally efficient welfare program gives everybody in need a chance to earn what he needs. He is not reduced to the status of a beggar, because he gets nothing for nothing.

He contributes to a central storehouse during his earning years. He can draw from that bank when necessary.

When not otherwise employed there is always work he can perform on the Church farm or in the storehouse.

I recently visited the vast storehouse in Salt Lake City where food, clothing and other essentials are available, made or grown by Mormons as part of their regular welfare tithe. It's a huge "supermarket" which dispensed 1½ million dollars worth of groceries last year with no cash register. The goods there cannot be bought, must be earned.

New York City alone anticipates a million persons on its welfare rolls within a year. That means one-in-eight New

Yorkers will be parasites, living off the taxes of the other seven.

Mayor Lindsay proposes the classic politician's solution, a bigger welfare budget. New York City next year will spend more money on welfare than on schools. Relief rolls continue to grow throughout the United States twice as fast as our population is increasing.

While so many Americans are banging on your door demanding something for nothing, we need to examine this Mormon example of how it once was and can be again.

Unwed mothers are neither rejected nor encouraged. They are provided at-home employment. Or they may live and work with a Mormon family.

The elderly and the handicapped are likewise usefully employed.

2,600,000 Mormons fast one day in each month. Food money saved that day is contributed to the general welfare fund.

Thus the bedridden or the disaster victim suddenly needing cash for medicine, rent or utilities can seek help with dignity because each has prepaid his debt.

Anyone who might become a chronic idler, required to work on the Church's hay ranch or in the flour mill or cannery or in making clothing at homes, learns the joy of accomplishment.

They gladly escape what the Bible calls "the curse of idleness."

Proof of this is the fact that Mormons who could be freeloaders aren't. They have a choice between taking Government welfare—picking your pocket—or, under the Church's self-help program, working for what they receive. With only the rarest exception, *they prefer to work!*

Please, Uncle Sam, we'd *really rather* do it ourselves!

DILUTED RELIGION UNINSPIRING

Every generation of students sometimes violated the rules. This generation is first to repudiate the rules.

A generation ago violated moral standards; today's young reject the standards themselves.

A generation ago jobless men might have demanded jobs; this generation many demand to be paid—work or not.

Clergymen, long the accepted authority on right and wrong, now preoccupy themselves with right and left.

Some branches of Judaism have practiced activism far longer than the Christian faiths which have recently interested themselves in extra-religious activities.

Rabbi Arthur Hertzberger is himself an activist, advocating withdrawal from Vietnam, etc., but he concedes it is not good for the churches to get thus involved in secular matters. "The very moment that clerics become more worldly the world goes to hell all the faster."

Paradoxically, much of the clergy is turning away from what we used to call "fundamental religion" at a time of increasing hunger for it.

There is a human craving for something transcendent. Religious tradition for thousands of years knew the meaning of life and the purpose of death and the individual's proper place in the here and in the hereafter.

Now a vacillating, contradicting, codeless "modern" church

106

has compounded our confusion and left, in the place it once filled, a vast dark emptiness.

Church involvement in civil affairs is not unprecedented. During the Buchanan administration the churches were divided over the issue of slavery.

Usually our churches injected themselves only where issues of morality were debated. Today's activist churchmen presume to prescribe law, diplomacy, welfare, civil rights. The World Council of Churches in convention in Sweden in 1968 overwhelmingly supported young men who resist the draft "for particular wars."

If churches were made stronger by this extra-religious involvement, it could be defensible. On the contrary, church membership, which soared in the 1950's, is stagnating in the 1960's.

A Gallup survey shows ten years ago 69% of Americans thought "religion is increasing its influence." Today 57% say it is "losing its influence."

Professor Will Herberg of Drew University believes that the explosion of new scientific knowledge—the vetoing of old scientific truths—has caused doubt about religious and humanistic preconceptions. We've lost our rudder.

So the hippie protests that each of us has a right "to do his own thing."

That's what Hitler was doing.

HOW MUCH TO REAR A CHILD?

Hey, Uncle, how much does it cost to rear a child?

You allow us taxpaying parents only $600 a year to feed, clothe, house and train a youngster.

Yet to feed, clothe, house and train a youngster in your Federal Government Job Corps you spend $7,000 a year!

Now, which is the correct figure? Either we're allowing you too much or you're not allowing us enough.

You allow taxpaying parents $600 deduction for the care and feeding of each child . . . yet under the Cuban refugee program, you assume minimal upkeep requires $1,200 a year. If the Cuban boy or girl is attending school, an extra $1,000 a year.

How come you short-change the home-folks?

In the austere environs of a federal prison, you have discovered that it costs to maintain one person with no frills, no luxuries, and no borrowing dad's car—$2,300 per year!

By what rule-of-thumb do you estimate that Mom and Dad can do it for one-fourth that amount?

Under Social Security, you will pay $168 a month to maintain the elderly. What makes you think we can maintain our young on $50 a month?

And Uncle, your VISTA program (Volunteers in Service to America) spent $3,100,000 this last fiscal year to turn out only

202 trainees. That indicates that the cost of maintaining and training one youth for one year is more than $15,000!

Then how come we taxpaying parents get an exemption of only $600 to maintain and train one youth for one year?

Or let's see how much you spend upkeeping one youngster in military uniform. Housing, $55.20 a month. Food, $30.27 a month. Clothing upkeep, $4.20 a month. That comes to $1,076.04 a year.

How in the world do you expect parents to provide all these things, plus clothes, recreation, books, medicine for $600 a year? With your own figures, you admit it can't be done.

It is possible, Uncle, that you expect us parents to manage more efficiently than you, because we usually do.

With all our expenses, we American individuals have more than enough savings to offset our debts; you don't.

With all our prosperity, you, Uncle, are still spending per year 2.9 billion dollars more for relief than during the depths of the depression.

It may be that you are uncommonly extravagant.

However we try to rationalize and explain you and excuse you, it is still a hurtful affront when you allow us hardworking, dues-paying home-folks only six hundred dollars a year to rear a legitimate child, while you, under ADC, will pay more than $800 a year to upkeep an illegitimate one.

INFLATION FEELS GOOD—IS DEADLY

The house is burning, but it feels so nice and warm.

Every nation in history died worrying about the wrong things. During the much recorded decline and fall of Rome, Romans were anxious only about the Huns and Vandals who were nibbling at the fringes of their empire.

But Rome was done in—from within.

Today's wise men are warning us about "inflation." Our ten dollar bill lost four cents in buyability one recent month.

The dollar bill will be worth three cents less this year, at least.

The end result of a dollar worth less and less is a dollar that is worthless.

Each great nation state which sought to spend itself rich, spent itself poor.

You know this. I know this. The President knows this.

Yet we will not heed what history or they try to say. Because inflation is almost totally painless.

President Franklin D. Roosevelt said: "Any government, like any family, can for a year spend a little more than it earns. But you and I know that continuance of that habit means the poorhouse."

President Harry S. Truman said: "In a period of high prosperity it is not sound public policy for the government to operate at a deficit."

110

President Herbert C. Hoover said: "The geometrical increase of spending by our governments—federal, state and local—is called 'dynamic progress.' It is, in fact, 'progressive dynamite.' "

Recently the lid blew off wholesale prices. You'll feel that at retail shortly.

Already our Government has had to increase the interest on United States savings bonds, because our dollar is eroding so rapidly that investors were getting out less value than they put in!

A combined Economic Committee of Republicans and Democrats in the Congress is in total agreement: Inflation is here now and something must be done about it. But what?

Because inflation is mostly painless.

We can't blame the politicians. The last time one of them tried to campaign on a platform of hard dollars, federal frugality, working your way, nothing for nothing—five-eighths of "we, the people" voted against him.

There is the rub. We're in a crashing airplane, but with a cheerful pilot.

It's Federal Government, shoving more and more paper dollars on the inflation fire. But it feels so nice and warm.

Inflation is almost totally painless . . . Cancer.

NO PILL FOR GONORRHEA

Saddest and most painful side effect of the "new morality" is venereal disease. The pill does *not* prevent *that*.

A frequent hangover from sexual permissiveness is gonorrhea.

Atlanta estimates five cases for every hundred residents.

Los Angeles County Health Department has hired hippies to spread the word among that city's unwashed.

Miami's director of venereal disease control says, "We have bankers and even physicians infected."

Dr. William Brown of the National Communicable Disease Center in Atlanta says, "More Americans contracted gonorrhea last year than measles; gonorrhea is now out of control!"

The *Wall Street Journal* questions medical men as to why. Most cited two main reasons: Sexual promiscuity is encouraged by birth control pills. Also the new strains of gonorrhea, brought back from Asia by servicemen, resist our drugs.

A military doctor guesstimates that one in four of our soldiers in Vietnam, Thailand, Korea and the Philippines will contract gonorrhea this year and 30% of those will not respond to injections of penicillin.

They will be given oral doses of tetracycline drugs—which can have bad side effects.

In the early 1950's there was much talk that modern drugs had virtually eliminated this disease. They hadn't.

In the years following the Big War there was an increase in gonorrhea, but usually a shot of 600,000 units of penicillin was more than enough to cure it.

Earlier this year one student took 418 million units of penicillin—five times the amount usually needed to cure pneumonia—but the gonorrhea bugs survived.

Because women suffer no pain in the early stages of the disease, some medics estimate that 90% of infected women do not consult doctors.

They backtracked on one case history in Atlanta and discovered one sixteen year old girl in a suburban high school had infected ten male classmates and they, in turn, had spread the disease to three more girls.

If the facts about gonorrhea, openly discussed, are frightening—that's good. My own dear widowed mother may have made many mistakes in rearing her children, but somehow she managed to implant a terrible fear of the personal humiliation and physical "brain-consuming effects" of social disease.

I'm convinced that, during the undisciplined years, that fear was a potent deterrent to promiscuity.

Some high schools are trying to educate young people to the increasing hazard, but 85% of our nation's high schools are making no such effort. In many instances educators are overruled by parents who protest public discussion of this "sordid" subject.

The National Communicable Disease Center in Atlanta has awarded grants to 25 medical institutions for new studies on gonorrhea. Until they discover some remedy far more universally effective than any now available, the hazard remains.

If samplings can be projected nationwide, ten million Americans—one in twenty—will be infected with this disease this year.

OLD SOLDIERS VALUABLE CITIZENS

There's criticism in Congress of military men on retirement pay accepting civilian jobs with the government and thus collecting from the government two monthly checks. It's entirely legal, but the House Manpower Subcommittee in December 1968 heard its own staff director imply there's something wrong with any business which would retire a man one day and hire him back the next day and pay him two salaries.

Is there?

Isn't this a new era?

The civilian tradition of our country has been modified. As far ahead as anyone can see, there will be a continuing need for the military to man our ramparts. Generations heretofore were characterized by a wonderful, free-wheeling aloofness from foreign entanglements.

British boys played soldier; American boys played cowboy and Indians.

British dads encouraged "a tour in In'ja"; American dads wanted Junior to take over the family business.

We rallied 'round the flag and fought when we had to. But between wars, soldiers were second class citizens—a uniform was not even welcome in proper society.

Today our confrontation with other isms is less acute, more chronic.

Today our military services require, demand and get many

of our most talented technicians. We gird ourselves for nuclear-age warfare with highly sophisticated weapons and with highly skilled, carefully trained men.

You and I profess to know these things:

That we are no match for our adversaries in masses of marching men

That only technology can save us

That technology requires our most respected technicians in uniform

That a military career now demands compensation and commands respect.

Though we know all these things are incontrovertibly true, yet everything our military men learned in history books, in the Academies and since, is countermanded by antiquated civilian preoccupation with bayonet war.

A General from another age, commanding Selective Service, proclaims, "We can get all the men we need . . ."

Military men are taught that wars are to be won.

Civilian superiors insist that the goal is the fifty yard line.

Now, when antiquated regulations prescribe premature retirement, our most esteemed citizens are too often shunted aside, shushed and relegated to the back of the bus.

It's been the law for only one year that military men can draw both retirement pay and a civilian government paycheck simultaneously.

Before you get sold the notion that it's somehow wrong, evil or unfair for ex-military men to keep working, let's consider the alternative: If you tell a retired military officer that his considerable experience and his mature judgment and his invaluable administrative talent must be turned out to pasture . . .

We lose more than he does.

TEACH A MAN TO FISH

Young man, if you have any guts you'll get into business!

You want to solve poverty problems, it's business which produced on 7% of this earth's land more than half of this earth's wealth.

You're interested in the public welfare, it's business that provides seventy-two million jobs. It's business that packs every factory parking lot with a rainbow of recent models. And it's business which finances the inevitable freeloaders.

So you want to do something worthwhile for your fellow man? Get into business.

You see a lot of young people these days fanning moonbeams with their hats—chasing hither and yon at taxpayers' expense—trying to help somebody else.

They play patty cake with poor people: "I'll hold your hand, then you'll feel better."

Hold hands, nothing! You want to develop the underdeveloped, give them a job!

You hear social-minded beatnik types professing to prefer some ism other than ours. They're the underdeveloped ones. Anybody who wants Government to take care of him hasn't been weaned yet.

Our American ism, with 6% of the world's population and

7% of its land owns 71% of its cars, 56% of its telephones, 83% of its TV sets, 90% of its bathtubs.

It's up to us who know better to stand up and challenge those mop-topped nincompoops and their assinine theories.

Don't let *factions* claim credit for America's magnificence. Labor did not build the United States; management did not build it; Republicans didn't build it and Democrats didn't either.

It was We, the People of the United States, who put rivets in the American dream. Every man and boy of us who dug the holes and set the forms and poured the mix and, one bucketful at a time, built skyscrapers over the blacksmith's shop.

Each American, seeking to outreach the other for a place in the sun, caused us all to grow tall.

You talk about a "happening." Youngsters with guts, in Junior Achievement, have recently started 5,746 companies in 410 communities. Junior Achievement businesses are set up like America's Corporations, with boards and officers, and they issue stock and they organize and they produce—then they market and sell and keep records and sell and pay taxes and sell and sell and sell. And 80% of those businesses profit and prosper!

President Richard De Vos of Amway Corporation is a sparkplug in Junior Achievement. He remembers he and Jay Van Andel started the Amway business in a home basement seven years ago and today it's a multi-million dollar enterprise providing employment for 80,000 people! "Yes," says De Vos, "Horatio Alger still lives in this country! The American dream is still good."

All we need is more people with more guts. The horizon has never been so limitless. Half the products we'll be using 20

117

years from today aren't even in the dictionary yet! Our nation needs nothing to keep on keeping on except more people with enough guts to get into business.

It's an old American proverb: Give a man a fish and he eats for a day; teach him to fish and he eats for a lifetime!

CAN A GOOD BUSINESSMAN
BE "GOOD?"

When Angel and I first came from the "little" into the "big leagues," we were warned by the old pro's that we'd have to be prepared to compromise some principles.

"It is necessary in the big city," we were confidently advised, "to entertain associates, employers and prospective employers. This necessarily involves wining as well as dining them if you are ever to be accepted."

Nonetheless we didn't and somehow we were.

Admittedly, my profession affords a mite more independence than most. How about the others? Is it good business to be a "good" businessman? What would happen if a Christian gentleman tried to conduct a business without compromising his convictions?

That question has been answered in a Gold Rule book for businessmen written by one of them, Mr. Marion Wade. His book is called, "The Lord is My Counsel." It relates the manner in which he and his associates built a multi-million dollar business—with the Lord as their "lawyer."

Where it's S.O.P. in industry to get on the telephone for an attorney's verdict on what's right and wrong, Marion Wade gets on his knees.

It is a fascinating book, in shirt-sleeve English, about an ex-ball player's adventures as a Daniel in a den of bulls and bears —as a "good" businessman making good!

Realistically recognizing that the fledgling Scripture reader may get discouraged and confused by all the "begats" in the Bible's beginning, author Wade recommends that business-men start with the familiar gospels by Matthew, Mark, Luke, and John.

"Even if his knowledge is limited to what he has seen in Bible-based movies or what he reads in newspapers around Christmas and Easter, at least he will have something familiar to start with. Knowing a little about what he is reading will be important in sustaining his interest during the first few weeks of developing the habit of Bible reading daily."

Mr. Wade advises "a chapter a day" to keep the Devil at bay.

The author is a friend, business associate and golfing companion of mine. If I have made his words sound stuffy, the fault is mine, not his. Marion Wade, in person and in print, is an uncommonly cheerful practitioner of all he preaches.

The author did not have such a dramatic Christian experience as the Apostle Paul who "got knocked off his horse on the road to Damascus." Between his conversion in an evangelistic meeting and his total commitment several years elapsed. It was following an accident which almost blinded him that the author was reading from Joshua when Chapter One, Verse Eight seemed to him a personal command:

"This book of the law shall not depart out of thy mouth, but thou shalt meditate therein day and night, that thou mayest observe to do according to all that is written therein: for then thou shalt make thy way prosperous, and then thou shalt have good success."

For Marion Wade, it came to pass.

I keep remembering our nation prospered most when we lived closest to the Biblical admonition that "believing on these things, all else shall be added unto you."

WHAT CAN YOU DO? PLENTY!

Americans, periodically acutely anxious about our multiplicity of problems, frequently lament, "But what can I do? I'm just one person." Let me tell you what just one person did.

Mrs. Mattie Rice Coney is a schoolteacher in Indianapolis. Teaching thirty years in slum schools convinced her that "slums are made by people and people, properly motivated, can clean them up."

She organized a nonprofit "Citizens Forum" in 1964 and set out to *clean up Indianapolis.*

Mrs. Coney is a Negro. She can talk to today's slum parents in the same schoolteacher language she addressed to many of them as children: "Get down off the white man's lap and walk like a man."

She says, "You can't act like an inferior and then demand respect as an equal. Too many of our people are noisy, boisterous, vulgar and common in public places."

Mrs. Coney said, "In many areas it is our people who have torn up the grass and broken down the shrubbery and torn up the house and made the neighborhood a slum. Bad neighborhoods develop because individuals who live in them fail to do what they can. It doesn't make any difference if they let you move from a dirty, noisy, rowdy neighborhood in one part of town into a white man's neighborhood in another part of town if you take your sloppy, dirty, noisy, rowdy ways with you. *You don't get culture in a moving van!"*

So while the eyes of the news have been gravitating toward more sensational "demonstrations," one Indianapolis schoolteacher has gone to work to brighten the corner where she is.

House by house she petitioned slum residents to organize a "block club," to meet once a week in somebody's house. Expecting a gripe session, they came. Instead they got a top-sergeant treatment from Mattie Coney: "No matter how poor I am I can be clean and neat and have pride in myself."

To each block club she assigned homework: Clean up the house, including the yard. Plant flowers. Involve the children; what they clean up they'll not be so eager to mess up.

By the second year, 1966, the clean-up drive launched by this uncommon woman cleared from the homes and yards and streets of Indianapolis's slums 40,000 tons of trash.

The 1967 cleanup cleaned up 181,000 tons in 28 days.

Subsequently the clean up effort has pyramided to demand more pick-up trucks. Increasing numbers of block clubs are proudly competing with one another.

Dr. Kenneth Wells of Freedoms Foundation, Valley Forge, Pennsylvania citing Mrs. Coney for her self-help slum-clearance, said, "That word 'pride' is the key to her success. Cleanliness begets pride and pride begets more cleanliness; all that's necessary is to get the ball rolling."

By brightening her own corner this dedicated schoolteacher's efforts have mushroomed from a local project into a nationwide campaign.

With the Freedoms Foundation acting as a catalyst "Help! Mayday!" encourages civic groups across the country to Clean up America.

Mrs. Coney says the project has no end. "Our migratory population requires a sustained effort by each block club to get newcomers to match our efforts, teaching them that a good city begins with each of us—paying his bills—keeping up his property—disciplining his children and himself. We Negroes want into the mainstream of America? All right. But the current is strong out there; it's going to take effort."

IF I WERE THE DEVIL

If I were the Prince of Darkness I would want to engulf the whole earth in darkness.

I'd have a third of its real estate and four-fifths of its population, but I would not be happy until I had seized the ripest apple on the tree.

So I should set about, however necessary, to take over the United States.

I would begin with a campaign of whispers.

With the wisdom of a serpent, I would whisper to you as I whispered to Eve, "Do as you please."

To the young I would whisper, "The Bible is a myth." I would convince them that "man created God," instead of the other way around. I'd confide that what is bad is good and what is good is square.

In the ears of the young married I would whisper that work is debasing, that cocktail parties are good for you. I would caution them not to be "extreme" in religion, in patriotism, in moral conduct.

The old I would teach to pray—to say after me—"Our father which are in Washington . . ."

Then I'd get organized.

I'd educate authors in how to make lurid literature exciting so that anything else would appear dull, uninteresting. I'd threaten TV with dirtier movies, and visa-versa.

I'd infiltrate unions and urge more loafing, less work. Idle hands usually work for me. I'd peddle narcotics to whom I could. I'd sell alcohol to ladies and gentlemen of distinction. I'd tranquilize the rest with pills.

If I were the Devil I would encourage schools to refine young intellects, but neglect to discipline emotions; let emotions run wild. I'd designate an atheist to front for me before the Highest Courts and I'd get preachers to say, "She's right!"

With flattery and promises of power I would get the courts to rule what I construe as against God and in favor of pornography. Thus I would evict God from the courthouse, then the schoolhouse, then from the Houses of Congress. Then in His own churches I'd substitute psychology for religion and deify science.

That way men would become smart enough to create super weapons but not wise enough to control them.

If I were Satan I'd make the symbol of Easter an egg . . . and the symbol of Christmas a bottle.

If I were the Devil I'd take from those who have and give to those who wanted until I had killed the incentive of the ambitious. Then my police state would force everybody back to work.

Then I could separate families, putting children in uniform, women in coal mines and objectors in slave-labor camps.

If I were Satan I'd just keep on doing what he's doing.

APRIL IS SOCK-IT-TO-ME-TIME

Federal Government spending has increased ten billion a year since 1965.

The White House blamed "the war." The Congress protested, "We've reduced expenditures to the bare bone."

"Let's see.

Your Federal Government spent 11.2 million dollars to subsidize art: to poets to write poems, novelists to write novels, to painters and sculptors to paint and sculpt, to undergraduate architects to study abroad.

Your Federal Government last year spent four hundred thousand of your dollars to purchase one thousand TV sets "to send abroad."

$208,741 of your dollars went to the Zuni Indians to teach them how to improve their jewelry business, though the Zunis have been doing a $2 million a year jewelry business for many years.

The Federal Aviation Agency desperately needed 106,000 of your dollars to have music piped into its offices in Hawaii.

Your tax dollars are financing a sobering-up station for alcoholics in Poland, a survey of husband-wife relationships in Israel and an archeological program for Yugoslavia.

You are financing a neolithic excavation in Poland, a study of old metal-working crafts in Pakistan and a study of the behavior of elephants in Ceylon.

The University of Texas got 89,000 of your tax dollars

to study sea breezes. Stanford got $41,000 to study "decision making in small groups."

The National Institute of Health spent $28,755 to study "changing patterns of Moslem family life."

So voluminous are the budgets of many federal agencies that members of the appropriations committees of the Congress can give each only the most cursory examination.

I lacked the time necessary to sift those volumes; I am indebted to Editor Jameson Campaigne and his Indianapolis Star research staff for culling this sampling of figures.

This is a perplexing problem for any President, any Congress. The bureaucracy has become so gargantuan that sifting, sorting and separating essential from non-essential expenditures is almost impossible.

Lyndon Johnson, forced by Congress to reduce Government spending in exchange for a tax increase, ordered "percentage cuts off the top" in each department. Thus it was left to the head of each department to cull and cut.

Immediately, of course, there was vociferous and valid objection from some Congressmen:

"You can't reduce the number of air traffic controllers when we have more air traffic to control!"

There were similar objections from enough departments so that Congress ended up re-instating most of the cuts the White House had ordered.

Thus we end up with bigger than ever budgets for such non-defense departments as Agriculture, Commerce, HEW, HUD, Interior, State Transportation, Treasury, GSA, Civil Service, EEOC and USIA.

The situation is not hopeless. The new Nixon team even has some examples worth emulating.

The heads of the FBI and the Passport Office have affected economies despite expanded activities. One of those Administrators is a woman; the other is a very uncommon man.

NEGROES AND INDIANS

In the early American slave states, the law provided for the welfare of the slaves.

The constitutions of the slave states generally specified that the slave owners must provide their slaves adequate housing, food, medical care and old age benefits.

The Mississippi Constitution contained this additional sentence: "The Legislature shall have no power to pass laws for the emancipation of slaves . . . (*except*) *where the slave shall have rendered the State some distinguished service.*"

Again: The slave was guaranteed food, lodging, medical and old age care—but the highest honor the state could bestow for distinguished service was *to set a man free from this security.*

The state's highest reward was to give a man the personal responsibility to find his own job, to pay his own way, to look after his own welfare.

Eventually the slaves were set free—free to earn money they could keep, to build or buy their own houses, to arrange for their own medical care and to save for their own old age.

Then they weren't slaves anymore.

On the other hand, consider the American Indians.

The Indians we made permanent wards of the government. Them we gave "security." The American Indians we placed on reservations, assigned 13,000 federal employees to look after them. That's one federal employee for every 30 reservation Indians.

The Indians became steadily less self-supporting.

Today the average American Indian—once so virile, strong and self-sufficient—would likely die of starvation unless fed by the government.

American Negroes, who were slaves just one long lifetime ago, are today mostly self-supporting, self-respecting, responsible.

The evolution I have just described—progression on one hand and retrogression on the other—has nothing to do with the color of a man's skin or the shape of his cheekbones.

The Negro was free to work or loaf, to starve or to win a potful.

The Indian was secure. There was no reason for him to educate himself or to learn to manage his own affairs or to be productive. It's not his fault, it's ours.

Just as it is going to be our fault if we let our leaders repeat this tragic error on us.

There are those today who think Americans are too ignorant or too worthless to be trusted with our own destiny. They are convinced that they would starve in the streets unless Government looked after our welfare.

Welfare! Man this is what American blacks were freed from a hundred years ago.

When the politicians guarantee "free gifts" and we rise to the bait . . .

When the politicians write laws "for your own good" whether you like them or not . . .

They are offering the rewards of *1862!*

A free meal, a free roof, free medicine, a guaranteed job—and we're trapped into being somebody's slaves again!

TINY TIM IS REALLY SOMETHING ELSE

Tiny Tim, the entertainer currently performing before packed houses across the United States, looks like a skid row reject.

Gawky, disproportioned, disheveled, with an almost grotesquely exaggerated profile, he appears at first repulsive, disgusting.

With multiple voice inflections including an upper octave falsetto he sounds effeminate. Throwing kisses to the audience helps affirm that image.

Yet, in spite of a distasteful appearance and almost no apparent talent, Tiny Tim has made himself a star attraction. How come?

I had to sit through one of those hour-long concerts before I could comprehend the enigma: Tiny Tim really is something else!

In a time of sophistication approaching cynicism, when the young are expected to "keep their cool" no matter what, Tiny Tim has "blown his cool" and his contemporaries can make themselves comfortable again.

Let me say it another way. The "cool" generation was expected to remain imperturbable; that is a difficult and uncomfortable pose.

Their popular songs (those not screaming defiance) were

weighted down with a surrealism of broken promises, shattered dreams, disillusion—but so what? Who cares? What else is new?

Now along comes an image in their unretouched likeness—neither handsome nor conventional. He talks happy talk and sings happy songs resurrected from comparatively innocent vaudeville days: "Fill Your Heart With Love," "On the Old Front Porch," "Tip-Toe Through the Tulips."

"Welcome to My Dream," sings this absurd appearing yet curiously gentle man.

"Livin' In the Sunlight, Lovin' In the Moonlight"—lilting, frothy, fun-music.

Each phrase of the song may be interrupted with one of those fingertip kisses or with an aside, "God bless you all," or with some equally square and probably contrived compliment, "I love to sing for you in this beautiful city . . ."

Yet you watch the cosmopolitan audience respond with eager warmth and it becomes apparent that a generation of Americans went to "pot" when what they were really starved for was a chocolate soda with two straws.

Escape we sometimes must from the grim realities of winless wars abroad and endless strife at home, from the pressure for grades—academic, social or economic—from the demand for more dollars with less, from the staggering acceleration of the inevitable cancer of time.

From the spectre of so many things sinister this newest diversion is the least objectionable in a long, long while.

Indeed, what bouncy, bug-eyes, joy-filled Eddie Cantor was to a generation that was economically depressed, Tiny Tim is to a generation that is psychologically depressed.

Tiny Tim, the antithesis of everything "cool," is what his contemporaries would themselves truly prefer to be. He's

131

"what's next" after an era of rock music and ribald lyrics and everybody conspicuously denying any tender emotions and thumbing his nose at cornball sentimentality.

God willing, after Tiny Tim will come a further evolution, a logical renaissance of unashamedly romantic music and musicians.

50 YEAR LEGIONNAIRE

This year marks the Golden Anniversary of the American Legion. Last Veterans' Day I addressed Ohio Department Legionnaires. During the banquet fifty-year members were invited to stand.

They stood.

We applauded.

When they changed Armistice Day to Veterans' Day a few years ago in order to honor all of the living and dead from all of our wars, it seemed somehow to diminish the importance of the day rather than enhance it.

Or maybe our national allegiance has become diluted by international cohabitation.

Or perhaps the rudeness of reality has minimized the significance of what we thought was the war to end all wars.

Anyway, we may never again celebrate an old-fashioned Armistice Day with the joyful abandon of the men who really believed that they had made the world "safe for democracy."

What these survivors of the Meusse-Argonne and Belleau-Wood feel in their hearts . . . about their war . . . is still true. It was a better war . . . than any since.

The men who marched to the cadence of "A Long, Long Trail a Winding" through the mud and murder that was France in 1918 were marching toward something; they were marching toward home.

They believe to this day that theirs was the toughest war fought by the *best* soldiers for the *best of all possible worlds* . . . the world when they were young.

We of later wars must yield them this: They faced machine guns without armor. Poison gas was a reality, not a withheld horror. There were no PX, no troop rotation, no free tobacco, no insulated clothing, no sulfa powder, no morphine to minimize the agony of gangrene, no blood transfusions, no airmail from home and no air transportation back.

They came home to scratch for jobs without government help or handouts. No sooner did they get the jobs than they lost them in the Great Depression.

But these men had taken the toughest that war could dish out . . . and thus had proved themselves . . . to themselves.

So most faced the worst that came after with their jaws set and their sleeves rolled up and, asking nothing for nothing, fought back against economic adversity with the stubbornness with which they had vanquished a tyranny.

These men of Chateau Thierry are out of step today. For their ears still hear the different cadence of a distant drummer.

They don't understand the new ways which deliver Berlin to our enemies and wheat to our adversaries.

They don't understand police action which we are afraid to win and ashamed to lose.

They don't understand the cold wars and the little wars which harass us in unpronounceable corners of the world without cease . . . and with a purpose ill defined at best . . . comparatively meaningless . . . apparently endless.

They don't understand.

You'll see them around our Veterans' conventions . . . ill-at-ease . . . standing aside . . . watching the new breed through watery eyes.

Maybe they sit-out the parades . . . and maybe they drink too much.

Yet you may well detect in us younger bucks a hint of envy of these men of The Marne, The Ardenne and Verdun—and even the honored dead they represent.

They lost their lives but they won their war.

THE LITTLE RED HEN

Once upon a time there was a Little Red Hen who scratched about and uncovered some grains of wheat. She called her barnyard neighbors and said, "If we work together and plant this wheat we will have some fine bread to eat. Who will help me plant the wheat?"

"Not I," said the Cow. "Not I," said the Duck. "Not I," said the Goose. "Then I will," said the Little Red Hen—and she did.

After the wheat started growing the ground turned dry and there was no rain in sight. "Who will help me water the wheat?" said the Little Red Hen.

"Not I," said the Cow. "Not I," said the Duck. "Not I," said the Pig. "Equal rights," said the Goose. "Then I will," said the Little Red Hen—and she did.

The wheat grew tall and ripened into gold grain. "Who will help me reap the wheat?" asked the Little Red Hen.

"Not I," said the Cow. "Not I," said the Duck. "Out of my classification," said the Pig. "I'd lose my A.D.C.," said the Goose.

"Then I will," said the Little Red Hen—and she did.

When it came time to grind the flour, "Not I," said the Cow. "I'd lose my unemployment compensation," said the Duck.

When it came time to bake the bread, "That's overtime for me," said the Cow. "I'm a dropout and never learned how," said the Duck. "I'd lose my welfare benefits," said the Pig. "If

I'm the only one helping, that's discrimination," said the Goose.

"Then I will," said the Little Red Hen—and she did.

She baked five loaves of fine bread and held them up for her neighbors to see.

"I want some," said the Cow. "I want some," said the Duck. "I want some," said the Pig. "I demand my share," said the Goose.

"No," said the Little Red Hen. "I can rest for a while and eat the five loaves myself."

"Excess profits," cried the Cow. "Capitalistic leech!" screamed the Duck. "Company fink," grunted the Pig. "Equal rights," screamed the Goose.

They hurriedly painted picket signs and marched around the Little Red Hen singing, "We shall overcome." And they did.

For when the farmer came to investigate the commotion he said, "You must not be greedy, Little Red Hen. Look at the oppressed Cow. Look at the disadvantaged Duck. Look at the underprivileged Pig. Look at the less fortunate Goose. You are guilty of making second-class citizens of them!"

"But—but—but—I earned the bread," said the Little Red Hen.

"Exactly," the wise farmer said. "That is the wonderful free enterprise system; anybody in the barnyard can earn as much as he wants. You should be happy to have this freedom. In other barnyards, you would have to give all five loaves to the Farmer. Here you give four loaves to your suffering neighbors."

And they all lived happily ever after. Including the Little Red Hen who smiled and smiled and clucked, "I am grateful. I am grateful."

But her neighbors wondered why she never baked bread any more.

NO MORE RASPBERRIES

When hired hands cost more the farmer must mechanize to survive. If it's a crop which cannot be picked by mechanical hands, he must plow it under and plant something else.

Either way the farm worker is out of work.

It has happened to raspberries. Thousands of acres are being plowed under. As a food you can buy in the store these dainty, delicious little berries soon will be no more.

Extinction threatens plums and asparagus, though a new mechanical harvester may rescue asparagus.

It could happen to table grapes. A farm labor organizer named Cesar Chavez was determined to unionize California's grape harvesters. Unable to interest those free-wheeling migrant workers in paying union dues, he re-directed his campaign at the growers themselves.

Pleading the plight of the "poor worker," Chavez got Hubert Humphrey and the National Council of Churches and the AFL-CIO behind a nationwide boycott of all California grapes—unless or until the growers would agree to his demand for a *closed shop*—thus to force the grape workers into a union whether they like it or not.

The National Labor Relations Board decreed the secondary boycott illegal and ordered it ended. Grape growers got a reprieve. But this does not resolve the inevitable phase-out of farm laborers.

Here is the problem: You can train anybody in two hours to cut bunches of table grapes with hand shears. You can pay him $2.50 to $3.00 an hour plus California's fringe benefits including Workmen's Compensation, Unemployment Compensation and Health Insurance.

But you cannot afford to pay that man the four-to-five dollars an hour which a cement truck driver gets in Detroit. Grapes won't sell at five dollars a fistful.

Historically our farms have employed many men not otherwise employable. When they leave the farm and go to the city they go on welfare.

So lawmakers and unionists intent on driving farm wages higher, either by organizing the workers or by increasing the federal minimum wage, are penalizing the worker, the grower, the consumer and the taxpayer.

All farming will eventually mechanize. Leave this evolution to American ingenuity and it will take place gradually, painlessly.

But if crops must immediately and forthwith be harvested mechanically or plowed under, we will throw an additional army of willing workers out of work and nobody benefits.

Already we have idled thousands of former tomato pickers. Switching from hand picking to mechanical harvesting of tomatoes, we're getting 18 tons an acre where we formerly got 30 tons—but the grower can afford that loss better than he can afford the higher labor costs.

Handling potatoes is so expensive that we are now marketing more than half of that crop in some processed form other than fresh. Like raspberries, fresh, field grown potatoes may soon be a food of the past.

As consumers we can learn to do without fresh potatoes and plums and raspberries. But if we arbitrarily increase the wages of farm hands, it will cost them jobs, growers income and taxpayers a further increased welfare burden.

That, for a nation arleady neck deep in red ink, could be suffocating.

THE FORGOTTEN MINORITY

You talk about a disadvantaged, under-privileged, discriminated-against minority—how about our farmers!

Twenty years ago his tractor and trailer for cattle hauling cost the beef farmer $4,000. Today it costs him $36,000.

Twenty years ago he was selling a two year old steer for $25; he's still selling a two year old steer for $25!

Yet, despite this punitive squeeze, the farmer minority in our nation is disinclined to march on public buildings and burn flags and burn and loot other peoples' property.

Recently I visited Alliance, Nebraska. Everything is cattle in the sand hills. The largest of all consigned cattle auctions is in Alliance, often handling a bigger daily volume than Chicago.

There are wheat and beets and beans and such in Western Nebraska, too, but mostly it's cattle country.

Those rolling sand hills are dotted with thousands of lakes. You can punch a hole six or eight feet down most anywhere thereabouts and have water. The sand seems to hold the moisture in suspension, making for almost year long pasture land.

Alliance, Nebraska is a town of only 8,000 people—yet its prosperous downtown looks like a city of thirty thousand. Its airport has four nine-thousand foot runways and a first class fixed base operator and a big league charter service plus scheduled Frontier flights.

Eight thousand population, yet Alliance was the first town in the United States to install touch tone telephones.

Eight thousand population, yet Alliance has a sporting eighteen hole irrigated golf course. And an ultra-modern system of modular education.

Alliance, population 8,000, for all its big-city appearance, nonetheless sees its young people grow up and go away to school and not come home again for, as with many small towns, the young ones seek what they consider to be the greater challenge and opportunities of the brightly lighted cities.

Yet I saw an interesting reaction set in there during the days following the Democrats' Convention.

That awful orgy of ugliness in Chicago televised nationwide had at least one salutory effect: It reminded a lot of young folks in hinterland America how very rich they are.

And, of course, there are other fringe benefits of living in that rolling ranch land of reputation Hereford herds: limitless fishing, and hunting, antelope, grouse, pheasant, turkey.

But these hard working, dues paying Americans don't appreciate what they see through that window of TV.

They work hard and pay taxes and obey laws and live decently—and they resent what they see of those who won't.

Farmers won't riot.

Encouraged by Walter Reuther, the so-called National Farmers Organization has in recent years been trying to get farmers to strike, to kill pigs, to burn crops, to dump milk. But few do.

Yet, however slow they are to anger, our farmer minority has had a belly full of big city bellyachers who refuse to be weaned.

If I might presume to counsel the President, somebody must

come up with some specific alternatives to present farm policies. Those hard-handed cowboys and sod busters are slow to anger, but they're getting kind of tired of nice guys finishing last.

SURE CURE FOR PROSPERITY

The din of divergent opinions from Washington, D. C. and almost everywhere else indicates everyone has discovered the cure for everything else.

I have a cure for prosperity.

The secret formula I am about to reveal has been lying around unnoticed for many years.

I do not know how far back in history the principle was first demonstrated.

My source is France.

It constitutes a sure cure for prosperity.

It does not matter how long you have had prosperity; whether it is chronic or acute, it can be cured. Even a stubborn case, though it may take somewhat longer, can be corrected by the repeated application of this formula.

The remedy need not be applied by professionals. Amateurs can achieve the same results.

You can.

It is, in fact, such a simple remedy that you will wonder why you didn't think of it yourself.

But I don't think you did.

To my best knowledge, the first person knowingly to make use of this cure for prosperity was a Frenchman. He was not an economist. He was a portrait painter by profession.

The painter was sitting at a sidewalk cafe in Paris, sipping his favorite wine.

A wealthy builder had just given him an order for a portrait, and the artist was celebrating.

His small bottle finished, he was about to order another, when his eye fell on a headline of a copy of FIGARO at the next table.

The headline said: "Hard Times Coming."

Instead of ordering his second bottle of wine, the artist called for his check.

"Is there anything wrong with the wine?" the proprietor asked.

"Nothing wrong," the artist replied, "but hard times are coming and I must economize."

"Hard times?" said the landlord. "Then my wife must not order the silk dress she wanted."

"Hard times?" the dressmaker repeated when the order was cancelled. "Then this is certainly no time to expand."

"Hard times!" the builder said, when the dressmaker cancelled his building plans. "Then I cannot afford to have my portrait painted."

So he wrote to the artist and cancelled the order.

After receiving the letter, the artist was dejected.

He went to his favorite cafe to console himself with a small bottle of wine.

On a nearby chair lay the same copy of FIGARO that he had seen earlier.

"Hard Times Coming," the headline said.

This time he read the date.

The newspaper was ten years old.

MORE YOUNG AMERICANS

GOING TO POT

Young Americans are hearing many unpaid commercials "advertising" illegal marijuana. Several professors, a few politicians and some clergymen are agitating for legalizing its sale and use.

Recently, a Britisher with a quasi-official affiliation lending credulity to his recommendation, said he'd rather his own son smoked pot "than get his girl into trouble."

That father imagining his pot smoking son will be a safer escort—that's like sending lettuce by a rabbit!

It is a goofy code of behavior which lists a bunch of evils and then recommends one or another as the lesser of them.

It would seem that the goal should instead remain a sober brain and a healthy body and a respectable and respected girl friend even though some will always fall short of those objectives.

About marijuana: The evil inherent in all dissipation is that it compounds itself.

It's been said of martinis, "one is not enough; two are too many; three are not nearly enough."

That is the way it works. As the body seeks physiologically to adjust itself to accommodate the intrusion of a toxic, you develop a tolerance and thus require stronger and stronger doses.

146

Narcotics Commissioner Henry Giordana, says the consensus of medical men and lawmen is the same: "Marijuana, if not in itself habit forming, historically leads to the use of other drugs which are."

Officially our Bureau of Narcotics knows of 62,045 drug addicts in the United States. Admittedly that is a mere fraction of the users.

Judging from the increasing number of arrests, the use of marijuana is borderline epidemic. At one state university it's estimated that more than 50% of the seniors have tried marijuana and that "most of those have become regular users."

Our Pentagon reports 2.5 men per thousand in Vietnam have been "involved in marijuana investigations"; doubtless many more are bringing home the habit.

In Chicago and probably elsewhere a sinister deception: The bad boys who peddle narcotics are spiking their own stuff. Some Old Town Chicago marijuana pushers are slipping a mickey into their cigarettes, "dusting the grass" with heroin. The heroin hits the blood stream through the lungs. The purpose, of course, is to get hippie pot puffers hooked on harder stuff.

The crafty hoods who wholesale narcotics are willing to reduce their profits from marijuana sales in order to insure a future market of new addicts.

The user, without knowing how it happened, becomes helplessly addicted. Thus the merchandisers of "Acapulco gold" are intent on enslaving a generation of young Americans.

And a second generation! Eight hundred babies were born in New York City last year already addicted to drugs! They were the children of junkies, hooked by the drugs taken by their mothers!

There are richer than ever potential rewards for those who

abstain. When a large proportion of the population is anesthetized or narcoticized, they become less competition for the others.

More than ever there are advantages in self-discipline.

The more Americans who abuse their bodies and brains, the more room at the top for those who do not.

WHO PAYS BILLS WHEN DROPOUTS DROP OUT?

Everywhere we are hearing that today's young people are less interested in money, more interested in performing good works. They want "roles," not "goals."

Having watched their parents work harder and harder to pay taxes which soar higher and higher, frequently neglecting what the young consider "love" and "beauty" and "fun" . . . our flower children withdraw.

They see that money does not necessarily bring happiness and they proclaim themselves on a glorious quest for "real" values.

I can comprehend their disenchantment with the profit motive. Sometimes the "establishment," which they renounce, appears hypocritical and cumbersome and costly to me, too.

But when everybody becomes a dropout from this rude, ruthless, profit-motivated society—who's going to pay the bills?

The flower children are willing to use our streets and our sewers and our utilities. They enjoy our beautifully manicured public parks and they adore Palm Springs. They accept traffic control which makes intersections safe for their motorcycles.

When everybody stops working and earning and paying taxes, who will provide medication and hospitalization for accident victims and narcotics addicts and venereally diseased? When they collapse in some gutter crying for help—who will be there to help?

When the generation which deplores work and disrespects

money and despises authority gets pregnant—where are the doctors?

When they get hungry, where is the bread line? When they are mugged, where is the policeman?

For all these standby *services which none of us wants, and all of us need, cost money.*

It is an irrefutable law of this Universe that we get nothing for nothing; we cannot reap without sowing.

Personally, I think most of today's refugees from reality are not "idealists" at all; they are cowards.

Probably you and I growing up, with no depression from which to run scared, with Government offering to take care of us whether we worked or not—probably you and I might have been tempted to live on free love and free feed and freedom—like barnyard animals.

I thank God we did not.

It was each of us getting up earlier, working harder, loafing less, pushing ahead—it was we who created this unprecedented prosperity which these parasitic cowards—afraid to face the competition—are trying to drink up and shout down and throw out.

And I thank God, too, that those who are trying to stop the world and get off are a miniscule *minority* among today's school-agers. For everywhere I see them overwhelmingly out-numbered by Boy Scouts earning merit badges, Junior Achievers building businesses, newsboys out in the pre-dawn dark building character, legions of young salesmen pounding pavements and ringing doorbells, unapologetic and unashamed of the money motive which turns the wheels and buys the bonds and builds the machines and puts hot rivets in the dreamers' dreams.

It's individuals willing to go the extra mile who have built for us all a stairway to the stars.

ARE THE GENTLEMEN OF THE
PRESS PEOPLE-EATERS?

Twice in recent weeks segments of our press have been indicted for unbecoming conduct.

The Milton Eisenhower report on Chicago's convention-time rioting criticized the press in general and TV in particular for throwing gasoline on the flames.

"Camera crews did, on at least two occasions, stage violence and fake injuries."

Further, "Demonstrators did sometimes step up their activities for the benefit of TV cameras."

At the same time, the respected periodical, *U.S. News & World Report,* asks "Will the press be out to get Nixon?"

Just the premise that the press could or would is terrifying, but then the publication goes on to trace the antagonism of "elements of the press" back to Mr. Nixon's exposure of Alger Hiss in the 1940's.

"Mr. Nixon's struggle (with the press) continued through his days as Vice President and culminated in Nixon's public castigation of the press in his famous "last press conference" in 1962: "You won't have Nixon to kick around any more . . ."

Author Theodore White, in his book, *"The Making of the President 1960,"* refers to "Nixon's bad press," explaining that the reporters who covered Mr. Nixon during the 1960 campaign were "predominantly Democratic in orientation."

Nixon, as President, remembers, has let it be known that

151

he prefers to be quoted directly rather than to have his views paraphrased by reporters or commentators.

Nonetheless, Washington is rife with rumors that liberals in the press are "out to get Nixon."

The regular columnist for one liberal magazine admits that he may participate in the conspiracy. He says if Nixon takes a "conservative approach to Government the press will give him a hard time as, in our modest way, we may try to add to it."

U.S. News & World Report quotes a longtime Washington correspondent who predicts more political partisanship and personal opinion in the reporting of news, citing the performance of TV commentators at the Chicago convention.

"A new generation of journalists have come along who favor the John F. Kennedy type of politician. These journalists, who fancy themselves as intellectuals, have an aversion to the Nixon and Eisenhower types—because Nixon and Eisenhower are conventional American personalities.

"The idea of detachment and objectivity in political reporting is rejected by this new crop of journalists. They believe that the true criterion of journalism today is to become 'involved' in political and social movements."

If we who treasure the tradition of a responsible press here appear to hang our profession's soiled linen in public view it is not without purpose that we do. We would alert you.

The trendency which others are now noting, I have noted. With increasing persistency, news conference questions are designed to shape the answers; those answers which resist reshaping may not get quoted at all.

Is it therefore important for the reader increasingly to question that which he reads or the listener to question that which he hears or the viewer to question even that which he sees with his own eyes?

Yes.

THE LAW NOBODY LIKES

This is for every workaday American who is confounded by the complexity of a "simple" W-2.

Or for anyone who elects to take the deductions to which an honest taxpayer is entitled, yet must hire an accountant or a lawyer or both to compute his income tax responsibility.

On the historic meadows of Runneymede in England, the Magna Carta was handed to King John on the end of a sword.

"Sign on the dotted line!" And he signed.

Then and thenceforth, the Magna Carta denied to Royalty the right of unlimited taxation.

Never again could any ruler take from the peasant more and more and more until the tax total became 100% and the peasant was taxed out of all his private property.

Never again until us.

It was for the American people to become the first in history ever voluntarily to surrender their right to private property. We did it with an innocent sounding Constitutional amendment which says, "The Congress shall have the power to lay and collect taxes on incomes from whatever source derived . . ."

We forgot to put any limit on the amount to which we might thus tax ourselves. During the Congressional debate preceding passage it was deemed "inconceivable" that the entire tax would ever total more than ten per cent.

Today, with taxes averaging 35%, many economists agree that we are precariously close to the historical point of diminishing returns.

Historically, after a nation taxes its people more than one-third of their income, incentive is destroyed and stagnation ensues. Hard workers begin to work less hard. Momentum will carry such a nation for a while, but eventually it backslides into history's graveyard.

There are three reasons our nation's stifling tax system is overdue for a major overhaul:

One, we need a legal ceiling on taxes, so that we can never be taxed out of all private property.

Two, we need to encourage the industrious, not discourage them.

Three, the annual hassle has become so grotesquely cumbersome even tax lawyers can't keep up with the inconsistent and constantly changing tax laws.

I know the complexity is a pot of gold for bureaucrats and professional figure-hounds, but it adds up to an economic constipation which our nation cannot indefinitely afford.

It's not too difficult to foresee that we might one day have in the White House a dedicated desciple of REALLY BIG government. Before that time comes, We, The People, should insist on recovering our fumble by rewriting that Sixteenth Amendment. We must limit the total tax and, for goodness sake, simplify the bookkeeping part of it.

Every retired Commissioner of the Internal Revenue—as soon as he was out of office—has urged reforms. Let the President name them to a commission charged with destroying the Frankenstein Monster which threatens to overwhelm us.

THE PRICELESS IMPERFECTIONS

that make a house a home. . .

PROLOGUE . . .

It is the season of the year when we consider the incarnation. The night the long-sought light entered the world through the windows of a stable. Snug at our own warm hearthsides, we are closer to home at this season than at any time of the year. As my own appreciation of home was whetted by the proximity of Christmas I began to reflect on what makes this place more important than any other to each of us. What magic causes all men to gravitate irrevocably to that one mansion, house or hovel to which his heart belongs? Pondering this, I arrived at a very unexpected conclusion . . . that it is the imperfections that mean the most . . .

Home is the place where a man goes when he thinks he's off work.

A place where anything undertaken is interrupted. A thing with a pervious lid and a prodigal heating plant.

There accrues with age, to home and the man, a wealth of imperfections.

Home is a small stain on a breakfast room wall where baby once splashed oatmeal. Indelible. Irreplaceable. Home is an ancient, tattered kite tail tangled in a tree, a squeaky stair, a sofa coming unstuffed.

Home is a dented downspout; once a shiny fender bore a matching scar.

A knurled chair rung signed by a teething puppy.

A carpet stain . . . camouflaged.

A plywood magazine rack, hand-made. Inelegant.

A home includes a basement crypt for broken toys . . .

A garage . . . chronically untidy . . .

And an attic . . . dusty . . .

Repository for one box of old letters, frayed, faded, forgettable . . .

And assorted boxes filled with a wonderful, worthless potpourri of useless things that might come in handy . . .

And what's left of a ruffled bassinet.

Home is a weary refrigerator, grunting with each nocturnal start.

On a coffee table, a careless scratch that once brought tears to a bride's eyes . . .

The ill-fitting garbage can lid is dented from backyard service in the Cowboy and Indian wars.

The closet switch you've been meaning to fix because it doesn't always light when it clicks.

The corner of linoleum that comes unglued and the window that won't.

The arthritic door with the hardware like they just don't make anymore . . .

These make the difference.

A house you can build of steel and stone and trees and nails and pipe and plaster . . .

But it has to be broken in, sometimes up, to ripen.

A house is just a beginning.

An accumulation of material, tangible, seeable, touchable, memorable, priceless imperfections . . .

Make it home . . .

VOLUNTEERS MORE EFFICIENT
ALL FRONTS

I have always insisted that the good neighbor policy should start over here, not over there, that we should first be good neighbors over the back fence—then overseas.

Instead of telling the world how it should mind its business, we should show them by practicing good citizenship at home.

Because I am only rarely able myself to practice the home community involvement which I preach, Angel has.

With admiration and respect I have watched my own Phi Beta Kappa wife and comparably competent men and women serving on the Salvation Army Board and as officers of Infant Welfare and Mental Health and hospitals and the like. I have seen them tirelessly giving to these community and charitable efforts brainpower which such agencies could not possibly afford.

I have wished the Government might somehow similarly inspire men and women to donate their talents to Washington, D. C. as many did during the Big War.

As is, leaving the administration of government to bureaucrats, we pay so much for often mediocre personnel.

Please, I do not mean sweepingly to slur all Government workers. But the good ones know of whom I speak when I say that too often the taxpayer pays too much for too little.

To get capable people to give themselves to Government

157

service when they can make so much more money elsewhere might sound impossible except, as I say, in war time they do.

In community affairs, properly motivated men and women not only give their services without compensation but usually at considerable expense to themselves in time and money.

So it is possible.

During Fall, seminars are conducted at seven universities around the United States. Co-sponsored by the General Federation of Women's Clubs, the Sears Roebuck Foundation and the National University Extension Association, these seminars seek better ways of re-directing wasted woman power into channels of community betterment; they teach clubwomen who are already active "how to do it better," how to be more effective.

Why could not the Administration in Washington put less emphasis on handouts and payoffs and more emphasis on inspiring competent volunteers?

Instead of handing hush-money to street gangs, instead of heaping dollars on delinquents and worsening the conditions we are trying to correct, why could not the new Administration, riding the crest of public favor, call for volunteers?

In each community we know who the leaders are.

Any volunteer army can outfight mercenaries—in peace as well as in war.

Could not "civil service" become "a duty" and "an honor" as it was in the earliest days of our Republic? I believe it could.

I may sound overly idealistic in the present atmosphere of much callous indifference. Yet listen closely to the restiveness of today's young people. They are yearning to identify with a cause. Perhaps their passion needs only direction.

The very ones who now resist serving under duress and who appear only to want to loaf, might be first in line to work if the reward were something more than money.

PRIVATE SCHOOLS FLOURISH

For a hundred years the Protestant church and public education in the United States were intertwined and, most of us assumed, inseparable.

The Lord's Prayer and the Golden Rule were taught in almost every schoolroom every day. Traditional Christian religious holidays were observed in classrooms, school assemblies and extracurricular school programs.

Since the Supreme Court banned prescribed prayers from public schools, there has been a national revival of interest in private schools. Protestant schools are presently being organized at the rate of 225 a year!

Americans, hard taxed to support public schools, are willing to pay extra to provide for their children's education in a Christian environment.

Several factors contribute to this phenomenon.

Overcrowded public schools have motivated those who can afford it to seek the more personal teacher-student ratio of the smaller school.

Grotesque misbehavior, individual and organized, which now characterizes many public schools has alienated both students and faculty.

Private church-related schools heretofore could not compete in the open market against the higher teachers' salaries available in tax-subsidized schools. Now many teachers, some fear-ing for their personal safety, flee the blackboard jungle for the happier environment of a selective school. If there is less pay, there are more "fringe" benefits on a Christian campus.

Based on achievement tests, students of the CACS schools are academically *a year ahead of the national average.*

Years ago it was argued that students maturing in a sheltered environment would, like hothouse plants, be unprepared for the cold outside world.

Now more than ever more Americans are eventually realizing that it is in fact the public or state school student who is "over-protected." He is "sheltered" from religious instruction and exposed to all forms of non-Christian philosophy and behavior.

And the harvest from the bad tree is bitter fruit. Youth crime is increasing eleven times faster than youth population is increasing.

Further, each student who pays extra to attend a private school saves the taxpayer from $500 to $900 a year, depending on the school district.

Christian schools predate public schools in the United States. Now we are turning back the clock to the "good" old days. Christian schools are the fastest growing education movement in America. CACS *membership has doubled in the last two years!*

When Dr. Max Rafferty was California's Superintendent of Public Instruction, he had high praise for the Christian Schools: "Private and parochial schools stand as probably the greatest single road-block to the standardization of the next generation, because these schools are teaching what we now need to learn most: morality, decency, respect for law, courtesy toward others, love of country and obedience to God."

ARE YOU OVERDOSED WITH NEWS?

Up to a point you are enlightened by exposure to news; beyond that point you are likely to become depressed by it.

Dr. Heinz Lehmann of Douglas Hospital, Montreal believes that you are presently getting an overdose of news. He told a symposium on psychiatry that many of us are suffering a kind of "shell shock" from the "communications explosion."

With all communications devices now bombarding you with events, opinions, debates, trials, troubles and violence, Dr. Lehmann says you are in danger of becoming "over-stimulated with resultant exhaustion, social withdrawal, depression."

Other respected voices have recently blamed news media for causing unrest. Pollster George Gallup insists the "news media are too preoccupied with conflict and controversy."

FBI Director, J. Edgar Hoover, says "Professional demagogues, extremists and revolutionaries have learned that the news media—television in particular—are their most effective weapon to gain notoriety and to discredit law enforcement."

Violence is contagious. University of Tennessee research confirms that "laboratory animals react to watching violence by trying to join in it."

"Mice which witnessed violent action experienced a significant increase in the rate of release of a brain chemical that transmits nerve impulses, became excited and tried to join the fight."

161

Dr. and Mrs. Bruce Welch, with this research, have satisfied the National Academy of Science of the validity of the theory, long held by many sociologists, that *violence is contagious.*

Senate investigators satisfied themselves five years ago that "there is a conclusive relationship between juvenile crime and TV shows which emphasize crime and violence."

Semanticist S. I. Hayakawa told The American Psychological Association this year that, "Today's youth are the first humans ever to grow up having watched TV all their lives. Their rioting, drug taking, alienation and radical politics may all be consequences of this influence."

And although the TV industry has reportedly taken some steps to minimize violence, a recent survey of children's cartoon programs revealed an average of 8.5 incidents of violence per cartoon.

While television's comparative newness subjects it to a greater concentration of criticism, other news media competing for audience have sometimes been inclined to "dramatize."

With some experience in and understanding of all media—newspapers, radio and TV—I can no longer ignore the criticism.

But I am more anxious about some of the suggested remedies. Abuse of freedom inevitably results in more Government snoopervision curtailing freedom; already some are recommending press censorship.

The Pottstown, Pennsylvania *Mercury* recently shocked its 25,000 readers by publishing a "censored" edition.

All unfavorable news regarding federal, state or local governments was omitted. All unfavorable news from Vietnam was omitted; the spaces left blank. All unfavorable riot news from our cities was deleted. The editorials were impotent pap.

That pock-marked publication reminded those readers as no

other admonition could: There is something worse than news which arouses or annoys. The something worse is news you cannot trust. For it is behind that smiling front that dictators are spawned.

WILL ALL SQUARES PLEASE STAND UP

"Square," another of the good old words, has gone the way of "love" and "modesty" and "patriotism."

Something to be snickered over or outright laughed at.

Why, it used to be that there was no higher compliment you could pay a man than to call him a "square-shooter."

The ad man's promise of a "square deal" once was as binding as an oath on the Bible.

One of those ad men, Charles Brower, says he's fed up with this beat generation distorting and corrupting our time-honored vocabulary.

Some of what I'm going to say next he said first, but I second the notion.

Today's "square" is a guy who volunteers when he doesn't have to.

He's a guy who gets his kicks from trying to do a job better than anyone else.

He's a boob who gets so lost in his work he has to be reminded to go home.

A square is a guy who doesn't want to stop at the bar and get all juiced up because he prefers to go to his own home, his own dinner table, his own bed.

He hasn't learned to cut corners or goof off.

This creep we call a "square" gets all choked up when he hears children singing, "My Country, 'tis of thee . . ."

164

He even believes in God—and says so—in public!

Some of the old squares were Nathan Hale, Patrick Henry, George Washington, Ben Franklin.

Some of the new squares are men like John Glenn, Walter Schirra, Walter Cunningham, and Frank Borman.

John Glenn says he gets a funny feeling down inside when he sees the flag go by. Says he's proud that he belonged to the Boy Scouts and the YMCA. How square can you get?

A square is a guy who lives within his means whether the Joneses do or not, and thinks his Uncle Sam should too.

He doesn't want to fly now and pay later.

A square is likely to save some of his own money for a rainy day, rather than count on using yours.

A square gets his books out of the library instead of the drugstore.

He tells his son it's more important to play fair than to win. Imagine!

A square is a guy who reads scripture when nobody's watching. Prays when nobody's listening.

A guy who thinks Christmas trees should be green and Christmas gifts should be hand-picked.

And he wants to see America first—in everything.

He believes in honoring father and mother and "do unto others" and that kind of stuff.

He thinks he knows more than his teen-ager knows about cars, freedom and curfew.

Will all gooney birds answering this description please stand up? You misfits in this brave new age, you dismally disorganized improperly apologetic ghosts of the past, stand up!

Stand up and be counted!

You squares . . . who turn the wheels and dig the fields and move mountains and put rivets in our dreams.

You squares . . . who dignify the human race.

You squares who hold the thankless world in place.

165

RAILROADS COME BACK

How come almost every other enlightened nation is improving its rail passenger service while we are letting ours decay?

Our railroads have been phasing out passenger service as fast as the ICC will allow.

With skyways jammed and airports forced to curtail traffic, the need for alternative transportation is increasing. Railroads protest that passenger trains lose money, they can't afford the drain.

Recently the Interstate Commerce Commission issued an economic report contradicting that conclusion, showing that for each of the last eight years, *railroad revenue from passenger service exceeded expenses for passenger service.*

Additionally, the ICC says that during the past fourteen years—despite losses from 1954 to 1958 and again in 1967—passenger service more than paid for itself. Passenger revenues those fourteen years exceeded operating expenses by thirty-five million dollars!

The Association of American Railroads says it isn't so, charges the ICC with "financial chicanery," says the agency must be using "some kind of new math."

While this ancient debate drones on, Americans with a preference or a need for train travel are finding schedules reduced, passenger accomodations less attractive, services aboard declining or discontinued entirely.

Gallantly, some railroads have tried to hypo short-haul passenger service. High speed rail service between New York and Washington, operated by the Pensy, at 110 mph has cut rail time between those cities to less than three hours. (Counting travel time to and from airports, this is competitive with air transportation—and less costly.)

At the same time, the C&O-B&O, beginning January 1, 1969, serves complimentary meals to sleeping car passengers.

Conversely, however, the CB&Q wants to discontinue two passenger trains between Chicago and Kansas City "because the Burlington lost more than $282,000 last year on those two trains."

The Railroad's spokesmen note that competing Ozark Airlines, over the same route, has received federal subsidies since 1954 totaling more than five million dollars.

This—subsidy—appears to be the necessary inducement for which rail men are waiting.

Some of us who consider passenger train service essential to our wartime and peacetime mobility find no satisfaction in the name-calling between the AAR and the ICC. Railroads remain the most economic form of passenger mass transit. Railroads cannot be expected to perform this service as some sort of charity. And we cannot afford to allow more railroads to go bankrupt.

Senator Harrison Williams is sponsoring a bill which would authorize the Federal Government to subsidize commuter railroads. It would pay up to two-thirds of out-of-pocket operating losses.

The railroads would still have an incentive to make money on passenger service, but would be protected from losing too much on unprofitable routes.

Such encouragement might provide the incentive necessary to upgrade and re-popularize passenger train service. The Chicago and Northwestern over the past six years has modernized equipment, improved service, doubled its commuter traffic, is showing a profit.

Also, the new Canadian National Railways Turbo train has proved that when speed and luxury and convenience are combined and available, such service is profitable.

Senator Williams' subsidy may not be the whole answer but it's better than nothing. And we've tried nothing.

SEE HERE, PATRICK HENRY

Drive some two hours south from Washington, D.C. and you can disappear two hundred years into the past. Colonial Williamsburg, Virginia now is as it then was.

You'll park your car out of sight by the Inn and journey by carriage or afoot along cobbled streets to the grand Palace where the British Governors of the Virginia Colony lived and ruled and entertained.

Sit quietly on the vast porch of Christiana Campbell's and look out across the lawns to the Capitol Building and you might yet hear the eloquent Patrick Henry denouncing the Stamp Act before his fellow burgesses.

Then go inside to the table at which Colonel George Washington and young Tom Jefferson worried over pig roast and pumpkin fritters about the increasing tyranny of the Crown.

Then follow their footsteps up toward William and Mary College. You'll pass the apothecary shop and the bakery, the shops of the gunsmith and the harnessmaker, the cabinet maker and the wigmaker, the printer, the bootmaker and candledipper—each artisan dressed in the fashion of 1770, each shop open and displaying the same handicrafts produced with the same tools as were used then.

If two centuries seem long from where you now sit, it seems not long at all—in Williamsburg. Just three reasonably extended lifetimes ago young George Washington rode out to Carter's Grove plantation nervously to propose marriage—and was turned down.

He, after all, was a working man. In families of many children the perpetuation of influence required that estates be increased, not divided, by marriage.

There is no record of whether the young lady lived to regret her decision.

You'll be reassured by the scrutiny to which the governing House of Burgesses selected its members. Each had to be a man of absolute integrity with a personal history of civic involvement.

As you breathe the air of Colonial Williamsburg, living among the sights and sounds of that time and place where liberty was about to be born in pain, you share in and grow to love the gracious life and the gay Palace balls and the carefree countryside rides and you don't want to leave . . . you don't want to give all this up . . .

And then—and it happens to most visitors on the evening of the second day—the awareness strikes with a swift, sharp pain that all this is what these magnificent men of Williamsburg did give up—that we might be free from a foreign oppressor.

Colonial Williamsburg and its historic public buildings and private homes and craft shops have been preserved or restored under a grant provided by John D. Rockefeller, Jr. in 1926. For the remaining 30 years of his life he gave this project his personal attention. The serenity and character of the houses and gardens have survived the installation of the hotels, conference center and adjacent golf course.

Nowhere more than here have I felt the past brought to life. And from that experience in the then and there I return to the here and now with renewed reverence for our Republic which cost so many so much and a renewed determination to help seek and find and elect custodians competent to keep it safe from all enemies, foreign and domestic.

THE AMAZING AMERICAN

Mr. "Anonymous" has written some fine stuff. Doubtless he has valid reasons for not wanting otherwise to identify himself as the author of these next paragraphs. If he does want to, I'll be happy to introduce him to you. If he wants to remain "anonymous," his words are no less worthy. I may have spiked this with a paragraph or two of my own to make it long enough, but mostly from here on I'm quoting.

The amazing American whips enemy nations, then gives them the shirt off his back. He yells for speed laws that will stop fast driving, but won't buy a car if it won't do a hundred.

The amazing American gets scared half to death if we vote one billion dollars for education, but he's cool as the center seed of a cucumber about spending three billion dollars a year for smoking tobacco.

He gripes about the high prices of the things he has to buy. He gripes about the low prices of the things he has to sell. He knows the line-up of every baseball team in the American and National Leagues but doesn't know half the words in The Star Spangled Banner.

An American will get mad at his wife for not running their home with the efficiency of a hotel and mad at a hotel for not being homelike.

He'll spend half a day looking for vitamin pills to make him live longer, then drive 90 miles an hour on slick pavement to make up for the time he lost.

The amazing American will complain about his wife's cooking. Yet, on a camping trip, he'll eat half-fried potatoes, burnt fish and coffee made with gritty creek water in a rusty bucket and think it's "wonderful."

The amazing American will work hard on a farm so he can move to town so he can make more money so he can move back to the farm.

In his office he likes to talk about baseball, football, fishing. Out at the game or on the creek bank, he talks business.

He is the only guy in the world who will pay fifty cents to park his car while he eats a twenty-five cent sandwich.

An American likes to cuss his government, but he'll fight any foreigner who does. He has more food to eat than anybody and more diet fads to keep him from eating it. His is the most civilized, most Christianized nation on earth, but he dares not deliver a payroll without an armored car.

In America we have more experts on marriage than any other country in the world—and more divorces.

The amazing American allows enemies of his country to hide behind the Constitution while they seek to set fire to it. He's likely to fight them in Laos and tolerate them in Cuba.

He would not steal money from his neighbor, but he'll pay tax collectors to collect it for him.

He irrigates desert to make farmland, then puts the extra acres in a soil bank.

He spent 280 million dollars last year on tranquilizers—and an equal sum on pep pills.

He tosses beer cans out the car window, drops gum wrappers in the gutter, plants auto graveyards along the highways, hides a mountain or meadow with a billboard selling laxatives, then stands up at his civic club meeting and, with a lump in his throat, sings "America, the Beautiful."

Yet, for all of that, the amazing American is still a pretty nice guy.

Despite all that he is not—because of all that he is—calling anybody "a real American" is still the highest compliment you can pay.

THE BOY-MEN OF VIETNAM

Tracey Sublett is the son of an Abilene, Texas minister. He's right now a long way from 5205 Texas Avenue; he's somewhere in Vietnam.

From there, through a letter home, this Marine PFC has helped me to a better understanding of the beardless boy-men of Vietnam.

If there is such a thing as an "average" G.I., what's he like?

Well, in most cases he's unmarried. His only material possessions of value are an old car at home and a transistor radio over there. His world is filled with ugly smells and rock music, loud laughter and 105-millimeter howitzers and sometimes sobbing.

He's just out of school, received so-so grades, played a little football, has a girl who promised to be true and who writes— sometimes.

He has learned to swagger, swear and drink beer because it's cold and it's the thing for a boy-man to do.

He's a PFC with one year in and one to go. Or maybe three.

Back home he worked only when he had to, preferred

waxing his own car to washing his dad's. He works now. From dawn to dark, every minute he's not fighting he's working. It beats thinking.

He can dig a foxhole, first-aid a wounded buddy, march until he is told to stop or stop until he is told to march.

He has stood among hills of bodies and has helped to build some of those hills.

And when the somebody he knew was among those who had died, he has cried. And cried.

The boy who littered his back-home room with soiled stuff for Mom to pick up now has two pairs of fatigues; he wears one while he washes the other.

He sometimes forgets to clean his teeth but never his rifle.

He keeps his sox dry, his canteen full; he can cook his own meals, fix his own rips—material or mental.

He will share his water with anybody thirsty, split his rations with anybody hungry and throw you half his ammo if you're fighting for your life.

He does the work of three civilians, draws the pay of one, yet finds ironic humor in it all.

He has learned to use his hands as a weapon and his weapon as his hands.

He's smooth-cheeked, tousle-haired, tight-muscled eighteen fighting to make nineteen; then he's nineteen fighting to make twenty.

He's scared.

He doesn't understand fighting no-win wars in unpronounceable places with less than our best weapons with fat targets off-limits.

He doesn't understand killing communists in Vietnam and tolerating them in Cuba.

Word from home is almost all about the homefront struggle

among the Have Nots and the Do Nots and the Will Nots and the Wash Nots and the Work Nots and the Nut Nots.

So he grumbles sometimes.

But then he gets a night's sleep and a letter from home and returns from a paddy patrol still forked-end down and figures he's lucky. And he closes his eyes and thanks God and says a prayer—for us.

THE WORLD WITHOUT VIETNAM

Let's now try to envision our United States—without Vietnam.

With that mess out of the way, much ferment in the USA would subside. Many demonstrations and much mischief derive from opposition to this winless war. Hopefully young Americans, spared the spectre of involuntary military service, could be reinspired to uplift our homefront.

As despair is contagious, so is pride.

It's not too far fetched to imagine that racial tensions would subside in the esprit de corps resulting from a united effort to make our America the beautiful more beautiful.

Also, the erosion of our dollar would be retarded, conceivably reversed, when more of our dollars stay home, recirculating through our own economy.

However tardily, Official Washington is beginning to reflect a groundswell of grass roots "enlightened selfishness."

They call it "growing concern for domestic problems."

Sargent Shriver, when in Atlanta, said, "Americans today favor spending more money on our problems at home and not so much overseas."

Well, what do you know! You and I recognized more than ten years ago that foreign aid had boomeranged, that we should be husbanding our dollars, making the United States vigorous and strong.

177

The notion that we should try to cure Asia's ills when our own country's temperature ranged from turbulent to violent seemed to us nonsense.

Draining gold from our anemic reserves to support unworthy allies seemed to us suicidal.

At long last this conspicuous hypocrisy has penetrated the Potomac fog.

Sargent Shriver, with personal political ambitions, might be expected to start moving closer to the voters but, whatever his motivation, he's welcome to the ranks of what were once derisively called "isolationists."

Shriver told the Atlanta Press Club that most Americans have now "come to the conclusion that unless we make progress on the homefront it doesn't matter too much how successful we are in Africa or Asia or somewhere else. The voters will think we have gotten *too far away from our own knitting."*

He promises to circulate a pledge among Congressmen that "when the war in Vietnam is over, they will spend that money on the homefront."

What better argument is there for disengaging ourselves in Vietnam immediately—and for carefully avoiding any further obligations to inject our troops into the affairs of other nations.

With military intervention the best we can offer those other nations—as in Korea—is a perpetuated military police state. That sort of government is not worthy of Americans; ours is.

On the other hand, we can become again a lighthouse for the unenlightened if we revitalize the American ism and renew, renovate and redecorate our showcase.

TIME OUT IMPROVES STATESMEN

Statesmen, a few years out from office, seem to make so much more sense.

Listen to the post-term public utterances of Truman and Eisenhower: definitive, positive.

Delegates and eavesdroppers to last year's GOP Convention were dumbstruck by the increased depth perception of Tom Dewey. They said, "If he'd talked like that in '48 he'd have been elected President!"

Hopefully Nixon has similarly benefited from a few years in which to observe, assimilate.

God required of Moses forty years preparation for leadership.

Churchill was shaped for his "shining hour" by many defeats.

American history records many examples of men whose greatness was not recognizable at first. Lincoln's several setbacks are the classic example. History rewards persistence.

John Adams sought and lost the Presidency twice before winning it in 1796.

Jefferson, who lost to Adams, came back four years later to win.

John Quincy Adams lost in 1820, won in 1824.

Andrew Jackson defeated in 1824, elected in 1828.

William H. Harrison lost in 1836, won four years later.

Grover Cleveland, defeated for re-election, returned four years later to defeat the man who had defeated him.

Of course the formula is not infallible as William Jennings Bryan and Tom Dewey and Adlai Stevenson could attest. But, more often than not, those politicians able to pick themselves up after a knockdown, went on to win.

Arnold Toynbee observed that every political leader should have a few years of reflection, a period out of the public eye that he can spend coming to terms with himself and with the world.

Nixon has ripened. He speaks with more self assurance, more authority.

Why cannot we, collectively as a nation, pick ourselves up and dust ourselves off from the myriad defeats which we have suffered abroad and at home and go on with renewed self-assurance, toward an expanding horizon.

As individuals have surmounted setbacks, cannot we as a nation do likewise?

We've allowed lightning communication and transportation to over-involve us with the world to the neglect of ourselves.

A few years of enlightened selfishness could renovate our America the Beautiful and renew the esprit de corps which formerly characterized our now divided people.

As statesmen have been motivated by adversity to un-dreamed of heights, let us all now be!

LIBERALS TRYING TO "CAPTURE"
NIXON

When Conservatives lose an election they rush to congratulate the victor, retreat to lick their wounds, and wait until next time.

When Liberals lose an election, they "offer every assistance" and try to stake out for themselves at least one corner of the White House desk from where they exert continuing influence on the incumbent.

As they moved in on Eisenhower, they are now seeking to "assist" President Nixon in his appointments and decisions.

Traveling, it is difficult for me to pass a news stand without perusing the editorial pages to see what issues are of most local concern.

Inevitably I peek at my own column to see my name in print. Recently, characteristically, these columns have subscribed to the President's suggestion that we "pull our country together."

But elsewhere on the editorial pages and in prominent national periodicals I read so many liberal pundits who are already hard at work trying to pull Mr. Nixon over into their corner.

This is not intended as criticism of colleagues; I am criticizing me. So starting now I'm going to be a little less pull-together and a little more pull-away from those sore losers.

Mr. Nixon owes the Rockefeller-eastern-liberal-establishment nothing! They fought him at the Convention and they helped him not at all during the election. Nixon lost New York, and New England this election by a greater margin than when he lost it to John Kennedy.

On the other hand, those Conservatives who did deliver Ohio and Illinois and all those southern border states to Mr. Nixon—those to whom he truly owes his selection—deserve much consideration.

Recent days I hear and read so many seeking to convince the new President that he "has a mandate to adopt many Humphrey programs"—and perhaps appoint Humphrey to his official family—"because the election was so close." Rubbish. Kennedy "squeeked" in and nobody questioned his "mandate."

"Nixon must shift to the left," another insists.

Significantly, many demand that Nixon turn his back on the Deep South which voted against him but none I have read says he should reject the Manhattan Islanders who rejected him.

The post-convention Nixon-Rockefeller shotgun wedding was an understandable political expedient.

Indeed, I am sure Mr. Nixon is genuinely determined to try to keep his party together and pull our country together.

This will necessarily require some accomodation.

My fear now is that he will listen to the concerted voice of his enemies to the subsequent neglect of his friends.

It is because Mr. Nixon's historic image is "conservative" that the liberals are now making such a concerted effort to influence him thataway.

It will be easiest for him to yield rather than suffer the criticism which the eastern liberals are able to mobilize against any who dare to oppose them.

Mr. Nixon, therefore, is going to need all the encouragement he can get to stand by what most voters considered to be his own personal principles.

Whatever other interpretation anybody tries to put on the returns from the recent election, this fact is incontrovertible: The liberal ism was rejected. In fact, by the combined Nixon-Wallace turnout, it was overwhelmed!

THE NIXON SMILE

"There are smiles that make us happy!" Yes, by George, there are. And if the turned down mouth of the most of us is ever to turn up again, we need a smiling example.

There is no sharper contrast between the present President and the former President than this: The one who's incoming is more outgoing.

Lyndon Johnson was almost always caricatured sad of eye and long of face. His imitators have perhaps overworked the line, "I come to you with a heavy heart." Yet that was his inescapable public image.

Mr. Johnson, known to be an admirer of Lincoln, may be an unconscious imitator of the emancipator. Addressing a farewell meeting of black members of his administration, Mr. Johnson said, "There will be a lot of bloody feet on the long road to equality."

Whatever kind of leadership that was, it was not inspiring.

How sharply this contrasts with Mr. Nixon's confident, affirmative, "close ranks, pull together, resolve problems, follow me, show the world" leadership.

When Mr. Nixon introduced his Cabinet on a nationwide telecast he appeared refreshingly youthful, poised, assured. He smiled easily, naturally, confidently.

It could be argued that Lyndon Johnson was weary from the tedium and complexities and frustrations and from the sheer weight of all that responsibility. But mostly what I am describing here are the contrasting personalities of these two men.

We needed a boost for our sagging spirits in the early 1930's. President Herbert Hoover, however capable he was otherwise, could not provide the psychological lift we needed.

FDR did.

The smilingly confident countenance of Franklin Roosevelt perhaps did more to disperse the depression's dark clouds than did all of his legislative acts put together.

FDR was able to steady our trembling hand on the eve of a great war with the firm admonition that, "We have nothing to fear but fear itself."

Sir Winston Churchill, whose presence ever exuded confidence, could promise his people nothing more than "blood, sweat and tears," but with his bulldog jaw stuck so confidently in the face of fate that the words of desperation had the ring of victory.

Similarly, none can over estimate the reassurance we all derived from the famous Eisenhower smile. His West Point classmate and lifelong friend, Earl Shaeffer said it: "Ike's grin is far more eloquent than he."

It does not have to be a grin. General Douglas MacArthur imparted the same confidence with ultimate dignity: "I shall return!"

Confidence is contagious and we need that now.

If this smiling President can disengage us from the foreign involvements which have contributed so much to the divisiveness within our own country . . .

If this President can sustain his clear-eyed optimism and deliver on his announced objectives . . .

It's going to feel real good again to be an American.

SIZE OF SHOES

Mr. Nixon's new shoes are bigger than his feet. No disrespect meant.

No man ever stepped into those shoes and found they fit right off, because never in history of America have we elected a man that size.

We elect men our own size.

Then one of two things happens: The man grows until he matches the magnitude of his responsibility, grows into those big shoes, or else he remains a little man and splashes around conspicuously until folks feel sorry for him and tell him to go get some shoes that fit him.

The Aura surrounding that high office has us awed.

We are inclined to believe that all Presidents have been intellectual giants, men of great stature and accomplishment. So we expect perfection. We mustn't.

Zach Taylor, the twelfth man ever to try on those shoes, actually appeared ridiculous in them.

He'd never voted in his life, had no interest in national affairs.

When they asked him was he a Whig or a Democrat he said he didn't rightly know.

When the Whigs nominated him anyway, and notified him by mail, he refused to pay ten cents due and sent the nomination back—unopened!

186

Mrs. Taylor smoked a corncob pipe in the White House, and the straw carpet in the Blue Room was one big stain of tobacco juice when Millard Fillmore took over in 1850.

Zach Taylor never did fit those shoes.

Go back a piece.

Take Van Buren, suave and clever diplomat. When they auctioned off his household goods later the carpet was threadbare in front of the mirror where he'd practiced his speeches.

Good talker, but he let the collector of the Port of New York run off with a million taxpayers' dollars.

Then came Harrison, William Henry Harrison. Whigs picked old Harrison because he had no ideas which could either interest or infuriate anybody.

He caught cold during his own inaugural address and died thirty days later.

He hadn't much time to grow, but he'd never have fit those shoes.

John Tyler tried them on then, but it was no use, no use at all.

Give you an idea, when John Tyler left office he couldn't even get a job to make a living. Finally went to work on a road gang and kept a village pound where he attended stray horses and cows.

No, John Tyler never fit those shoes.

I think history agrees Lincoln did—though not at first.

Homely Abe Lincoln, inside one term and one month and ten days, grew into those shoes and left indelible footprints along the Potomac.

Or, you take Andy Jackson, number seven man in the lineup of Presidents, first one from west of the seaboard.

He'd beaten the British at New Orleans, but I don't know that he'd ever distinguished himself otherwise until 1829 when the frontiersman moved into the White House.

Mr. Jackson's feet grew fast. He fired all who were lax in public or private relations. Eighty-seven employees of government had jail records. Out they went. Ten employees of Treasury were short in their accounts . . . Out!

He was a capable President. Yet, when he was elected, he had read only one book in his life, "The Vicar of Wakefield." No advanced education. He spelled Europe, "Urop." His grammar was frightful and he believed the earth was flat. But he was an incorruptible judge of right and wrong and he grew into those shoes and wore them well for two terms.

When Richard Nixon inherited those shoes, they hadn't shrunk any. They loomed frighteningly big. But the shoes already have begun to feel right comfortable. Mighty short growing time. Something of a record.

Americans, maybe we have the makings of a good President. Quite possibly a great one.

MR. PRESIDENT,

PULL US BACK TOGETHER!

Mr. President, you have been elected by a majority of American people. It was not the people of some other nation or of all other nations who elected you; you were elected by "us"—spelled U. S.

Your oath of office binds you to preserve, protect and defend "us" against all enemies, foreign and domestic.

You sought and got our votes to govern us. Your first obligation is to us.

Since the dawn of the so-called "nuclear age," some American Presidents have allowed themselves to become preoccupied with what our enemies might do or what our Allies might think.

We must assume that those previous administrators were scared. Thus they signed promissory notes binding us to forty-two other nations.

Indeed, your predecessor Lyndon Johnson once said, "Ten hours of the day out of fourteen I spend on the world—Latin American, European problems, Vietnam, relations with the Soviet Union . . ."

This preoccupation with other nations and their problems has left our own neglected homefront a chaotic shambles; we are now in worse trouble than are many of them.

Mr. President, come home.

Our American dollar, once a bulwark for all the world's

189

currencies, is eroding so fast and supported by so little gold that last year some foreign countries were refusing to cash dollars for American tourists!

Winless wars, waged in defense of unworthy governments with less than our best weapons for a lesser objective than victory—such wars are unworthy of our sons and our enlightened sons know it!

Big Government, buying votes with promises of "something for nothing" and "social equality" and "guaranteed security" —promises which no government can keep—fostered inevitable disillusionment and ultimate rioting.

There is but one way, Mr. President, that you can pull us back together: Make our American ism worthy of respect. Ultimately, if you do that, you will also re-win the admiration of the world. But put "us" first.

During your campaign, you promised "to return our nation to its rightful position of leadership . . ." I'm not sure what you meant by that.

The best city administrators are those who don't want to be Governor. The most effective Governor is the one who is not out running for President.

Right now we need a President of the United States who will give the United States his full time!

We were leaders of this world for most of a hundred years before we annointed ourselves its policemen. We "led" by being such a shining example that others were inspired to imitate us.

Then somehow we stopped leading and started meddling.

The father who is first and foremost good to his own family is inevitably a good neighbor.

He does not spoil them with unearned ease nor disillusion them with unkept promises nor sentence them to undeserved punishment.

190

Disengage us, Mr. President, from this suffocating spider-web of international involvements. You were not elected President of the world. You were elected President of the United States.

REQUIEM FOR A HEAVYWEIGHT

He was always the best hand we had around Reveille Ranch. Strong, good worker. We had scuffled before, as men will—Indian wrestling, arm wrestling, always seeking to best one another. But this time was different.

It was last Thanksgiving in the living room of the big, old ranch house. It was half-time in a televised football game. However it started, within minutes we were off the sofa and on the floor kicking off our boots, wrestling.

I still workout vigorously at the gymnasium, run three miles three times a week. So, though the lean ranch-hand was some younger, I must explain immodestly that I was always stronger and always emerged from our friendly tussels huffing and puffing—and victorious.

Even the family sensed there was something subtly urgent about this impromptu scrap. There were at first the usual admonitions from the ringside and jesting backtalk from the floor, but gradually my friendly adversary became conspicuously more determined.

I slid quickly from under his firm young body and took his right arm with me into a hammerlock. But, before I could apply the pressure, another arm—longer than I remembered—came from nowhere to break my hold and lock my head in an elbow vice.

I had unlocked his headlock before, lurching simultaneously to scissor his body with my legs. My legs, trained on gym weights and hundred pound hay bales in the barn loft squeezed his middle until he gasped and grunted—but he did not melt as he always had before.

Indeed, with his greater reach he unlocked my feet and, before I realized that he was imitating my own favorite maneuver, he had seized my foot, rolled me over face down on the floor, my both feet locked in a stepover toehold and it hurt. I couldn't let on how much it hurt. And my neck was aching from that earlier headlock. And my lungs were burning.

Our sweaty bodies had by now soaked our jeans; shirt buttons popped. What had begun as just another playful scuffle was now a grim test. No anger. No rancor. A test.

With all the strength I could muster, I banged one fist against the floor, bowed my back—caught a glimpse of the roaring fireplace—and others' faces. I wondered if they knew the quiet desperation of this drama at their feet. His weight on top of my back-bent legs was agonizing. I must hurl myself forward enough to break his tenacious hold—I always had—but I'd never known him to be quite so determined—or quite so strong before. If this last lunge failed, my shoulders could be quickly pinned for the decisive fall.

With all my residual strength, I tried—and failed.

My adversary, in that instant, could not help knowing that he had won.

Now it was necessary only for him to hold my locked legs with his, roll sideways, and shove my shoulders to the floor. He knew it. And I guess he knew I knew it.

How, in the years we had been scuffling, had my adversary grown so strong? And six feet six, a full four inches taller than I?

When had it happened that his prowess had surpassed my own? He had only to force my shoulders to the floor to prove there's a new champ at Reveille Ranch.

But you know what? He didn't.

With the bittersweet cup of victory in his grasp, he flung it away.

Instead, he said something about, "The second half will be starting . . . if we're going to watch the game don't you think we'd better call it a draw, Dad?"

He called it a draw.

MIRROR, MIRROR ON THE WALL

Pundits do not mean to be prophets of doom. News analysts are not really sadists who delight in accentuating the negative. Why, then, are we so often preoccupied with what's wrong?

We must be.

It is for us of this generation to analyze our mistakes and to recover our fumbles. As the coach looks at movies of yesterday's game, we must constantly research our errors so as to improve the status quo. That is why we necessarily concern ourselves with the debit side of the ledger.

Our youngsters, however, do not understand this critical introspection. To them, our constant harangue sounds pessimistic, defeatist, ominous.

Through this maze of admitted mistakes, they do not see a very fruitful future.

It is for them, therefore, that once in a while we must read aloud from the credit side of the ledger. They must not see our Republic and their prospects through the wrong end of the telescope.

To keep their perspective in focus—to keep them from figuring "what's the use, the country is a hopeless mess"—it behooves us sometimes to throw a little light on what's right.

Yes, there are four and a half per cent of America's workers not working. But ninety-five and a half per cent of America's workers are working.

There are right now as many Americans so ambitious that they are holding down two jobs as there are Americans with no job at all.

We're building nine million new cars a year.

No other nation in the world has such delightful problems as too many cars and too much food.

When you and I discuss these things only in terms of parking problems and surpluses, our most envied assets end up sounding like liabilities.

A hoodlum killing, a sex crime or a street fight make page one *because they are exceptional,* because they are not commonplace.

Fifty-one million Americans will go to church next Saturday or Sunday. That's not news.

One gun shot makes more noise than a thousand prayers. But it's not more important.

Our bewildered offspring need to know that.

Our dollar lost another half cent in purchasing value in 1968. That justifies some anxiety.

But American wage earners took home seven per cent more this year than ever before. That figure must be included in the audit.

The regrettable death rates from cancer and heart disease are debits, to be sure. To our everlasting credit, though, while America's pioneers expected to die at 27 we expect to live past 70!

Somewhere between the pessimist and the Pollyanna is the whole truth. If you can't see our America the Beautiful in the mirror, look at its reflection in the eyes of the envious.

For all our critics, this is still the only land in the world where people are standing in line waiting to get in, instead of braving stormy seas in small boats or climbing through barbed wire and over stone walls dying trying to get out.

If being an American is worth dying for—it's worth working at.

NO APOLOGY TO JUNE GRADS

I challenge those who can view only with alarm and who can see nothing more than just one big mess for our fine crop of young folks to inherit.

I challenge those who are so hang-dog apologetic about the "mess."

Nor do I think this particular generation has been discriminated against by either fate or their fathers.

Yes, it is an imperfect world. We have not done everything right and undone everything left.

We've not even invented a faucet that won't drip . . . or a swimming cap that'll keep your hair dry—or a car clock that'll keep running.

But . . . this is the Testing Time.

There is Communism threatening, but there has always been some ism threatening. Since wagon trains west—always some Indians of one tribe or another on the horizon.

There is erosion of our dollar threatening our economic solvency, but our dollar supply has always been too fat or too lean.

There is much too much wanton crime (increased 10%, 7 times faster than population) abroad in our land, but most of its increase is juvenile, not adult. And I'm tired of having you and your psychiatrists blame it on your mothers.

If some parents have failed to set an example for their children, so have some parents of every generation since Eve.

As I say, a newsman is more than ordinarily keenly aware of our society's short-coming. Still we must now and then examine the other side of the ledger.

The generations which spawned this upcoming one fought two big wars and assorted little ones to keep today's babies from being born slaves. We won those wars. We won those wars and accomplished that objective.

My generation dug itself out from under one of the most cruel depressions any nation ever survived and went on to rebuild the most powerful economy the world has ever known. Today's graduates are heirs to that legacy.

This much maligned generation has managed such medical progress that now—today—every young man and woman is reasonably assured of additional, useful, pain-free years of life itself!

We did that!

True, this school-age generation is handed a diploma with one hand and a gun with the other. I don't like that either.

But your daddies did not *invent* wars just to make you miserable. In the three-and-a-half thousand years of recorded history fewer than 8% of those years have been warless ones.

This earthly proving ground never has been all fun or all-easy for anyone.

Your great-grand-daddy did not find these streets paved with gold. He paved them.

However it appears on the TV westerns, the United States was not carved out of the wilderness. This America the Beautiful was scratched and clawed and chopped and sawed and dug out of the wilderness by barehanded men who asked nothing for nothing—who didn't expect freedom to be easy because they knew nothing worthwhile ever is.

What they did they did with courage and faith and with selfless concern for making this a better place for the sons and daughters who would come after them.

We don't tame the wilderness with an axe, anymore. But we joust with dragons and fight and pay and pay every bit as hard today—and with the same objective in view, young American: YOU!

So you get no apology, Young American.

You get for yourself a country mostly civilized, an economy still mostly free, a church door that's still open and unwatched, and you get a new mop and a new broom and a new hoe and a new chance to preserve and protect and defend those blessings—as we did.

And you know what? I'm on campuses two or three days every week. The goof offs notwithstanding, I've great admiration for this upcoming generation.

I sit across the dinner table from you every night that I am home. I've developed an abiding respect for what you stand for—and for the things you won't stand for.

It's you who convinced me that we all stand today on the threshold of the most fascinating, the most exciting, the most fruitful era in the history of the world.

Burris